Advanced Tennis

REVISED EDITION

PAUL METZLER

INTRODUCTION BY
JOHN NEWCOMBE

FOREWORD BY
ESCA STEPHENS
President, New South Wales LTA
and Australian Davis Cup Selector

Line drawings by Will Mahony

COLLIER BOOKS
NEW YORK, NEW YORK

To JACK CRAWFORD, prince of stroke-makers,
and to the game's Improvers—any age.

Revised edition

The Macmillan Company
866 Third Avenue, New York, N.Y. 10022

Advanced Tennis is published in hardcover by Sterling
Publishing Co., Inc., and is reprinted by arrangement.

Library of Congress Catalog Card Number: 68-18790

First Collier Books Edition 1972

Printed in the United States of America

Contents

Jack Crawford, Australia's great player of yesterday. In 1933 he came within one set of winning the world's first Grand Slam, and since that time no one has surpassed his effortless stroking and transfer of weight. This book, emphasizing strokes, is dedicated to him. Our picture shows him in perfect balance and almost at the end of one of his free-wristed Continental or English-grip forehand drives, in this instance played across the front leg. Such points, and many others, are discussed and illustrated in this book. Admirers of Crawford will claim that this picture was taken at the moment his sleeve button broke. He was as neat as he was bulky.

Foreword

This is the most interesting book on tennis I have ever read. Paul Metzler's early promise was once of great interest to me; choosing to make tennis a hobby, he has become a close student of it.

The backbone of tennis in all countries is made up of those thousands of players who compete in various matches, tournaments, and championships conducted at weekends. Here is a book written directly for such competitors by a player from their own ranks.

Its author is well qualified to write it. His record in this kind of tennis is too long for me to list here and I will merely say that I, among others, have had the pleasure of presenting him with various trophies from as far back as 1929 to the present time. That he can present his ideas and facts in a most workmanlike fashion you will soon see as you read his book.

Younger players are often uncertain, lacking experience. Here is experience, set down on paper.

There is much in this book to hold the attention of anyone interested in improving his tennis, whether it is competitive or social. Our leading players could well apply parts of it.

But I realize that to be read I must be brief. It is a grand book—one that makes a great contribution towards improving tennis wherever it is played, in method, character, and sportsmanship.

ESCA STEPHENS

Lew Hoad plays a backhand across the front leg.
(See text, pages 115–117)

Introduction

By John Newcombe

There are thousands of advanced players besides the professionals and internationals. If you play tennis regularly—competitively or otherwise—you are one of them. Tennis is not your living, so you play it on Saturdays and Sundays.

That's when Paul Metzler played his tennis: inter-club, inter-district, inter-state, even inter-Service for the Royal Australian Air Force, against all sorts, and in varying conditions.

His book is crammed with experience, and it hits the soft spot of many players in its first chapter. "Temperament lost more matches than strokes ever won," is an old saying. The author lays temperament's ghost in the most helpful way I have ever come across. He even makes you feel bored with it.

Tennis is booming in the States now. There are going to be more tournaments and more match players. "Advanced Tennis" is ideal for them, and for improving non-competitive players, too. I think the author is unique as a tennis writer; he has an eye like a hawk, and his instructions all come across so simply. He makes you take a deep interest in your strokes and in your knowledge of the game. This is just what you want the book to do anyway.

He knows you want to win, match-player or not, so he keeps to a winning theme—but you would be blind if you didn't see that between the lines you are also getting a lesson in competitive sportsmanship. This is part of the game, the way a sense of humour is part of life.

"Advanced Tennis" could improve you by fifteen a game. Sometimes you'll find the key in the stroke advice; or it could be in the "constant errors," or somewhere else, but overall I think it is in the confidence you will feel from having a grip on the whole situation.

I wish I had this book when I was trying to battle my way to the top. I apply much of it now.

CHAPTER ONE

Temperament

Strokes/Nerves/Concentration

Temperament, in one or another of its many demoralizing forms, has almost certainly held back your tennis in the past. Probably it has spoilt your chances of winning many a match; perhaps it even clouds your future enjoyment of competitive tennis, particularly in singles.

Much of this has been needless. You should not be burdened with future worries. True, you cannot expect to become completely free of temperament overnight, but it is possible for you to reduce its effects to a minimum—to a manageable minimum where it becomes no more than a part of the game instead of something likely to break up your play on important occasions or at critical stages of a match.

Temperament is seldom discussed in books and when it comes up in conversation many a fallacy is accepted as fundamental. Let us take a hard look at temperament and really take it to pieces.

Essentially *match temperament* boils down to having confidence in your strokes. It is not hereditary. No one was born with a good or bad match temperament. It is not physical. No doctor could examine all tennis players' nerve-ends and select those with good and bad temperaments.

Reliable strokes lead to good temperament

Spectators watch a great trier getting ball after ball back into play, perhaps even with rather awkardly made strokes, and justifiably respect his fighting temperament. But when they admiringly mutter "Born with it, I suppose," they are

9

talking superstition. Similar remarks are made about the one-and-a-half-stroke player (limited to forehand and second serve only). This sort of player is willing to run miles during rallies (he has to run round his almost non-existent backhand), and he never serves double-faults on important points (no wonder, after the practice he has had with that second serve). So he tends to be credited with a "born" match temperament.

These types of players were not born with their determined match temperaments—they developed them. Further, their temperaments developed in this admirable way because whatever strokes they had, even if awkward or limited, were sound. If a player can rely on his strokes and expect them to go into court each time he hits them, he will develop a good match temperament.

Unsound strokes are behind poor match temperament

Now let's examine the players with poor match temperaments. There is the timid player who pats everything in an agony of tentative caution, and the nearer the crisis the more timid he gets. Have a look at such a player's strokes. Invariably they are so poorly made that if he hit the ball hard it might go anywhere. He has to hit softly and let the ball fall into court rather than aim it in. His strokes are shaky and so is his match temperament. But this does not prove that there is anything wrong with the man himself.

Another type on the same side of the coin is the brilliant player who is often erratic and sometimes cracks up badly. His flexibility gives him a wide range of shots, and his easy action enables him to get maximum power with little apparent effort. The general verdict on him is that he has every shot in the game and that on his day he is a world-beater—*but* "Must be something wrong with him. Must be his temperament. Born with it, I suppose."

Neglect the "born" part; we have covered it already. This type of player deserves more sympathy than any other, particularly if he is young, because he is the most misunderstood player of all. Sometimes he is even called a quitter when in fact there may be nothing at all wrong with his character. I believe that his erratic temperament stems from what are really erratic rather than brilliant strokes.

If we analyze such a player's game we see that it is not so much on the shorter, sharper volleys and half-volleys that he is erratic but mostly on the serve and on forehand and backhand drives. Here he usually has the technical (not temperamental) fault of not having his racket in line with the ball for a long enough distance. Notice, however, that these are the good old basic shots, thus strengthening the illusion that it is the basic man who is at fault. The pity of it is that the man himself comes to believe it. The truth is that his stroking is basically unsound, erratic play results, and an unsound match temperament inevitably follows.

At this stage you may question whether temperament follows strokes, and say that it's just as likely to be the other way round; in other words, that unless a player has a sound temperament to begin with he would be unlikely to develop sound strokes. This would put us back where we started, and still leave you with any doubts you may have had about your own match temperament.

It's not as bad as that. I don't say I can prove I am right, any more than anyone can prove whether it was the hen or the egg that came first. But there is strong evidence to support my view, and I'm sure that if you are worried about your own temperament, it's a view you would really like to share.

Strokes that affect your temperament

Here are two points from that evidence. First, if you are much stronger on one side than the other, forehand or backhand, ask yourself if, when the pressure is on, your temperament is unaffected no matter which side the ball is coming to. You will probably decide that your nerves are steadier on your stronger side.

Second, if you acquire some sounder strokes and a few

dependable aids to steadiness in various crises (which I hope to help you with later), then you will find that your temperament will improve. You can do something positive about it. On the other hand, it could never be suggested to anyone that he should first acquire a good match temperament; instead of being able to do something positive, about all he could do would be to wish for a miracle to happen.

As mathematicians would phrase it, match temperament varies in direct proportion to stroke-soundness. In other words, match temperament boils down to having confidence in your strokes. For your own future peace of mind I hope you agree with me. Competitive tennis becomes much easier when you do.

Nervousness

Nervousness exists; no one can deny it; it is a fact of tennis life. We will look at whom it affects, what its place is in relation to the rest of your game, and methods of cutting it down.

Nervousness affects all players keen to win a match that is important and likely to be close. It affects juniors, players in the prime of their tennis lives, and even older players, though only at times and to a lesser degree. It affects champions, even though these players have confidence in most of their strokes and therefore in general have good match temperaments. It particularly affects players who know they have a weakness in their game. Most particularly, it affects players who lack confidence in every stroke, unless, of course, they have already sunk into the state of despair where all other feelings are effectively blotted out. The only bright spot is that it also affects your opponents.

One thing to be completely sure about is that you are not alone. The fear that you are a nervous and cowardly person, a born loser in tennis, can be put right out of your young head. I know your head is young if you feel this way. It has to be. Older people know that we all tend to be faint-hearted and "steel" ourselves every now and then, sometimes to the point of being decorated in wartime. By and large we are content enough that way. If we sometimes have to brace ourselves to play a tennis match it is not the end of the world. The game is well worth it, and we can still enjoy playing it and coming back for more next week.

For all players—young, prime, and older—experience shows (though once again no one can claim to know) that nervousness in tennis has its greatest effect on those who are unsure of their strokes, not on those who for one reason or another may be expected to have worse nerves than anyone else.

Nervousness has its place in tennis matches, but it is not the whole game. To imagine that you will lose any future match solely because of it is a gross exaggeration. Do not overestimate it. Wouldn't you rather play someone you know you can beat and who is not nervous than someone whom you know is a nervous player but clearly a better one than you are?

Another thing about nervousness is that it need only be temporary. If at any stage in a match you get a sudden feeling of safety or certainty in your strokes, nervousness will disappear. This point may occur in the warm-up Be conscious that there is such a point waiting for you. Look for it. And when it comes, hang on to it.

What has been said so far about nervousness may be enough for some people. Others, certain that they are really bad cases, may regard it as a prelude only and be waiting for me to produce some specific methods of cutting it down. I will try to oblige.

Traveling light

Always "travel light." Never boast that you can beat so-and-so any time, that you have a second-to-none chance of winning such-and-such a tournament before you have played the first round, or that you can always rely on a certain shot. Avoid boasting and thus shed the extra strain of making good your boast; modesty is the easiest policy.

Play each match as it comes without building the occasion into something that will be too big for you, or for any other normal man. Don't be overworried before the first match that it would be a disgrace to lose in the first round. In the final, give no thought to the fact that if you win you will be the title-holder, or will have won the event three times running, or whatever else it may be. If such thoughts are uppermost in your mind in a match, all you will be wishing for is its victorious ending, and you will hardly be able to hit the ball properly *during* the match.

Avoid dwelling on your weaknesses. You have balancing strengths to even things up, so think more about them. And not only in your strokes. If you have naturally fast reflexes, for instance, it is better to think you are quick as a cat than nervous as a kitten. Remember that when a glass is half empty it is also half full—always. And in any game where confidence is an asset, optimism is a more realistic attitude to adopt than pessimism.

Travel light. It is my guess that the well-known Harry Hopman sees to it that as far as possible his players always do. And this could well be one of the secrets of his success.

Attitudes players adopt

Some people follow the philosophy of openly admitting to themselves that they are nervous, and then determining to go through with it anyway. This amounts to a challenge, which is what they like. They become interested in the challenge, and the greater the interest the less room there is for actual nervousness.

Others employ strong self-control. They refuse to recognize nervousness even to themselves, and maintain an outward manner of everyday calm. Some keep a poker face. Some become taciturn and grim, some even aggressive. Whatever attitude they choose or force themselves into, there is less room for nervousness.

You might prefer to adopt the attitude best expressed as: "I'm still here—he hasn't beaten me yet." This at least guards against a restless night and the fate of being beaten before you start. You might decide that you are going to hustle your opponent right from the start, so that he will be the one who makes a fair number of errors early in the game. This admittedly is court tactics, and I mention it only as an example of concentrating on something constructive about the match instead of waiting around, increasing your nervousness. Overcoming nervousness has to be combined with something—anything at all, so long as we don't just wallow in it.

I once knew a contradictory individualist with a careless and offhand manner who was a strong and efficient match player. He told me matches petrified him so much that when he began one he always pretended to himself that the match already had been played and that he had been beaten hollow —that he was just playing a set or two to see if he could give the other man a better game. This had once happened a long time before and he had adopted it as a system ever since. He admitted that his system was defeatist nonsense that had absolutely nothing to recommend it except, as he so modestly added, that it always helped him to enjoy his matches and to ensure that he played at his very top.

Some of us with more conscience and rectitude than others may think this man too evasive to be either admired or followed. Perhaps, but at least he kept on playing competitive tennis, which is a long way better than giving it up and turning to golf—on a Sunday afternoon, all by yourself, and not even counting the strokes. A conscience is a good thing to have, but don't be too hard on yourself all the time.

Eliminating crisis points

Another method of reducing nervousness is similar to the old maxim of "taking care of the pence and letting the pounds take care of themselves." Applied to a tennis match, it means that you try to win every point and leave it to the umpire to decide who has won such incidental things as games, sets, and matches. That is the system in outline, and I think it is worth expanding in some detail.

Refuse to consider even the start of your match, let alone the final result. As far as you are concerned the next time you play will be in the practice warm-up before the game, and there you will see how your strokes are and perhaps if you can start to get on top. All deliberate thought stops there, and you look forward with interest to this warm-up alone.

Do not waste the warm-up. See that you have at least as many practice serves or overhead-action hits as your opponent and try to win every rally you can, without making it too obvious. You can't very well practice your accuracy by continually aiming for the sidelines and sending the ball out of your opponent's reach, but you can get this practice very satisfactorily by returning each ball exactly back along its line of flight towards you. Just as batsmen in cricket always follow this policy when they first go in against fast bowling, I have known more than one player who carried it on from the warm-up into the first few games in order to get a good feeling of control and to avoid giving an opponent those early-game birthday presents down between the tramlines.

When the game begins, then, just carry straight on from where you left off in the warm-up and try to win every point Right from the first one, for it is never too early to start winning. But do not worry over any you lose; your concentration is solely reserved for the next one, the one you are engaged in, the only one you can win that is in the present and not somewhere off in the future. In a tight game or close finish, limit your concentration even further—to each stroke in each point.

What you are doing by this method, of course, is spreading your nervousness thinly. Game, set, or match point becomes no more than just another point. You may object that this will make you somewhat nervous on every point, but it will not unless you really are playing very badly all the time; and at least it will prevent you from having sudden lapses at critical stages.

Again, if the match is interrupted or postponed at a critical point, worry over its outcome is left to your opponent and his supporters, while you have only one point on your mind—the next one.

However, this concept is not everyone's cup of tea. Some players prefer to relax and concentrate on freedom and loosening up in the warm-up. In the match they like to make their run when they feel most like it, instead of keeping their nose to the grindstone on every point. So suit yourself— tennis is free country.

It is a good thing to take nervousness, an old black hag if ever there was one, out of the unexplored cupboards of our minds and have a good look at it. But now that we have done that, I hope the whole business rather bores you and that you would much rather concentrate on your strokes and look forward to each match as a welcome opportunity to play them. When all is said and done, that is really my message.

Self-consciousness ruins your concentration. No player can afford it. If you are fortunate enough not to be self-conscious by nature, you should be able to rule it out of your tennis. If you do happen to be naturally self-conscious, face up to it and do something positive about it.

When it is time for your match and you are going on, walk firmly and grip the court surface. This is a positive statement of the negatively phrased advice not to stumble out self-consciously, feeling somewhat top-heavy.

If it is a cold day, blow into your hand to make it warm and pliable enough to feel normal on the racket handle. Take the balls, feel their compression and bounce them on the court surface to get an idea of what to expect. This is doing something useful, and is preferable to thinking that the presence of spectators (or someone special among them) is putting you off or to wishing that no one was there to see you.

Now let me repeat some of the advice about nervousness.

Neglect past errors, particularly the one on the last point. Eliminate thoughts of future errors and of how foolish they could make you look. Instead (positive once more) concentrate entirely on the point to be played. This concentration on the job in hand is the reverse of becoming self-conscious the moment you notice some of your friends or relatives arriving to watch after the game has started, particularly at an important stage of it.

Whenever self-consciousness intrudes, recognize it and at once substitute concentration. Decide what device suits you best and follow it determinedly.

Combating tension and casualness

No one likes feeling tense. It's uncomfortable; stiffens you up and takes away your power. It usually makes you play tentatively. About the only thing I cannot lay against it is lessening your concentration.

All of us would much rather feel casual, but feeling casual, though pleasant, is laden with traps. Carried on just a shade too long it can lose you the whole match or it can cause you to get such a fright that your attitude reverses itself into a bad case of tenseness. Either way you lose the confident stroking you had before.

It should be plain to you when you are letting your strokes become casual. There is, however, another form of casualness which can creep into your game without your being aware of it. This is casualness over the next point when you are already leading by one point. It happens more than you may think, its absolute zenith occurring in men's social doubles at advantage-server, where it is normal to see the serving side attempting the most adventurous shots. This is harmless enough, unless it becomes a habit and is carried over into matches.

Relaxed concentration is the ideal middle course between tenseness and casualness. Let's attempt an exact description of what it means.

Imagine your Thursday evening practice for Saturday's

match. You have a good court, good balls, an opponent of about equal standard, and there is just time for a couple of sets. You are trying to play as well as you can, with free stroking and no carelessness at all—in short, just as you would in a match, but with no strain attached. In such circumstances you are likely to play at your top form. This state amounts to relaxed concentration.

I doubt whether you will ever completely achieve relaxed concentration in any match that is evenly balanced and important to you, but it is well worth striving for. Try for it more in practice so that you will be more likely to get close to it in matches of all kinds.

Temper

Temper is not a match-winning attribute. Overcome it or you will be carrying a cancer about with you all your tennis days.

You may think you have a quick temper by nature and cannot really be blamed for your actions. If so, it is time you got things straight. Everyone has a temper, even the calmest looking people. A so-called quick temper is in essence no more than an uncontrolled temper, and in tennis this is not an asset.

Those who let their tempers run riot have never really been taught to control them (as distinct from being told—sometimes until their distracted elders are blue in the face). If this applies to you, learn to control it yourself. Temper is not the only thing you have. You have some character as well. So use it.

People who lose their tempers on tennis courts generally seek to justify themselves in several ways. They explain that they are only wild with themselves, and that no offense is intended to anyone else. They usually say they could scarcely play if they didn't let off steam once in a while. Some add that they cannot get worked up into a winning mood if they have to smile pleasantly all the time.

Displays of temper do give offense to others. Spectators

come to see tennis, not tantrums. If you put on a really bad performance your opponent probably would rather not be on the same court with you. Temper is never pretty.

If you specialize in a brand of temper that is mixed with toughness you may succeed in intimidating your opponent and making him easier to beat—but only if he is very young and inexperienced. After all, tennis is played with a soft ball and no one ever gets hurt, so who's frightened? It might have the opposite effect on your opponent. He might feel you would never act like that when practicing, no matter how seriously. He could put it all down to your nerves.

You do not have to smile politely all over the place, and you shouldn't try to. It can make you feel like a fool and perhaps even look like one, and it tends to make your play timid and your concentration sloppy. If you are the type who likes to play a tight, taciturn game when really trying to win, by all means do so. It never pays anyone, serious or jovial, to encourage his opponent.

Don't show your hand

Never treat your opponent unfairly in any way—quite apart from the ethics involved you will see a few good reasons why not in a later chapter—but you are under no obligation to do anything that will encourage him in the slightest. For instance, don't tell him as you change ends that he is playing well. Until then he may have been feeling unconfident about something as vital as his second serve. Give acknowledgment rather than fulsome praise if he plays a particularly good shot. Don't ever let him know that he has you worried about eventually losing. If this applies to normal players, it is doubly true for those quick-tempered people who give the show away so obviously.

Take as an example a situation where you are playing an opponent who has entered the event only for experience and does not expect to beat you. Suppose you are not playing very well and he manages to go along with you to about three-all. Stay with it and you will often find you have the set, because, not really thinking he can win, he lets you have a point or two for almost nothing, which seems to make just enough difference.

By contrast, imagine the position if at three-all you miss one and let your hair down in a great display of temper that can only stem from your badly needing that point. You startle your opponent straight into the realization that he has a real chance of winning this set, and at once you are playing a different man. You may as well have given him a glass of champagne.

In playing poker and making a one-card buy, do you let the result show?

Letting off steam

Perhaps as a last resort you choose to fall back on the actions of a few champions. You have seen some of them perform; you have even seen the best professionals let off steam and hit a ball over the stand. There was a period when "performances" were in vogue, but apart from that time the great majority of stars have not been performers. The older ones perform very rarely, not because they are older but because they have learnt that it spoils their own concentration.

Next time a professional champion lets off steam, take a closer look. Likely enough, the beautiful hit that goes right over the Kooyong stand and lands in Gardiner's Creek or somewhere will be made after everyone has been put into the right mood of expectation, and it will probably be made at the end of a game and just before the umpire calls for new balls. The spontaneous reactions from the crowd are cheers and laughter. The professional's incidents never leave a bad taste in the mouth. When a professional lets off steam it is pretty well-controlled steam.

Still not satisfied? Still want to be able to let off your own steam? Well, take a good look at yourself. You might be one of those players who fairly belt the ball into the back fence after you lose a point, but return at once to a careful and even anxious type of game. It could well be your own frustrating game that is really bottling you up inside. Improve your strokes so that you can play a lot faster with equal confidence. Then if you miss an annoying one you can press into the next rally and perhaps make your opponent set up a weak lob that you can come into and *bounce* over the back fence. I'm all for something like that.

And now I have had enough of it. If you still want to be a one-man Wild West show, go ahead. This book is trying to cater to all types, so I have included your case and hope you feel it has been considered fairly. I haven't at any stage suggested that you should behave like little Lord Fauntleroy. I admit that the killer instinct can be an asset towards winning. But while you're at it, you might as well be effective. Be a cold killer.

This should be sufficient dismemberment of temperament for almost anyone. From among the pieces lying about I think we can assemble the following picture:

• All aspects of temperament that adversely affect your play can be reduced in their effect.

• It is normally useless to follow a negative attitude such as telling yourself that you are not going to be tense. You should substitute some positive aim such as relaxed concentration, or anything else of your own invention.

• The most positive thing you can do towards achieving a sounder temperament is to develop sounder strokes, regardless of your grade or standard of play.

The complete answer as I see it—and with a nebulous affair like temperament it can never be more than a personal opinion—is to make your strokes sound and then add two things: clear knowledge of exactly what you are trying to do, and complete absorption in carrying it out.

The book now develops along these lines.

CHAPTER TWO

Watching and controlling the ball

"A good eye for a ball" / Long contact / The timing pause

If effective strokes are the basis of the whole game, it is appropriate to examine the basis of the strokes themselves.

Coaches and champions alike are unanimous that the first thing for a beginner to master, and the most essential point for a champion to observe, is: *Watch the ball.* Older players, parents, elder brothers, everyone around you—all express this fundamental in their different ways. A former Wimbledon winner says: "In preparing for a big tournament I spend the whole of the first practice session in concentrating on watching the ball." A saddened coach says: "The first thing learnt, and the first thing forgotten."

This leads straight to the first point I want to make. Whereas just about everything else in tennis should be learned and then done instinctively as needed (because too much thought and a fast-moving ball do not go well together), I think that watching the ball is not enough in itself. You have to watch it and be conscious of watching it.

This is something of a paradox. The most natural thing anyone can do on a tennis court, besides breathe, is to look at the ball, but it is by no means natural to watch it properly. This applies particularly to the forehand side, where your head does not turn round with your body and drop over the ball as it does on the backhand.

When you are aware of watching it, the ball looks clearer; some players even go so far as to say that it looks bigger. Quite apart from this, however, there is a bonus for consciously watching the ball—concentration on the job in hand.

The way to watch the ball *mentally* is consciously.

Watch the whole flight

My second point concerns the *physical* method of how to watch the ball. There's no mystery about it. You must watch it the whole way. Like many an answer given without reasoning behind it, this will probably make little impact. Here is an illustration of what I mean.

A well-known coach was once exercising about twenty juniors at Sydney's White City against a machine that knocked out balls at varying speeds and angles. Each junior had to play a backhand drive followed by a forehand volley, and all were going through the routine well enough except for one unfortunate young man who was wobbling his volleys into the net. The coach had to stop everything to concentrate on him.

"Get it *over*," he said.

The lad missed the center of the racket and the ball fell into the net once again.

"Watch the ball."

Same result.

"Watch it closely. Watch it right on to the strings."

Off the top edge of the frame.

"Put that racket down. Now catch the ball this time. Watch it go right into your fingers, for Heaven's sake!" Two dropped catches.

The lad started to tremble.

Suddenly the coach saw what was wrong. The lad was watching the ball with the rigidity of a mesmerized rabbit. In trying to watch it closely he must have foreshortened his focus to the last yard or so, and perhaps at the last fraction watched his racket head or his hand instead of the ball. Once the coach had him watching the ball the whole way his troubles were over, no doubt from that time to this.

Eyes tend to follow the ball less closely to the racket strings with forehand volleys. However, here Rod Laver punches one.

(See text, page 23)

Rod Laver drives a wide ball strongly down the line,
hitting outside the ball to swing it back inside the sideline.
(See text, page 32)

Watching the ball the whole way seems to take the speed off it. If you anticipate the direction of a shot, if you get behind the ball's line of flight early and watch it arrive, then even though the ball is traveling fast you sometimes get the impression that your concentrated vision has virtually stopped it just before you hit it. That is what lies behind many an older player's ability to see the ball well even though he may need glasses to read the telephone book. He doesn't do it from memory, as some people imagine. He knows *how* to do it.

A good eye for a ball

Disregarding the veterans, here is the general application: If you have what is known as a good eye for a ball this does not really refer to your eyesight but to the way you use your eyes. When people say that someone has a natural eye for a ball in any game he takes up, it really means that that person uses his eyes to the best advantage naturally. I hope this chapter adds you to the number of players who have "a good eye for a ball."

Next, you must have *ball control*. Without it you will never be able to string enough strokes together to have any worthwhile interest in position, tactics, or systems of play. Even an ability to see the ball so clearly that you can practically stop it is of little use if you cannot hit it with control.

If you haven't got ball control already you must acquire it, and I may as well say here and now that you can. Any one or two of the following sections may contain the clue you need.

Against an opponent of anywhere nearly equal standard to your own most of the shots you receive are not difficult. Even when you are overmatched your opponent's winners come more from his outmaneuvering you than from his sending over a stream of difficult shots that cannot be returned into play. If this were not so there would never be any rallies. Study it for yourself next time you play or watch.

Once you realize that most of the shots you receive are comparatively easy, more and more seem to become so. The next development will be that you make a lot of them easier, mainly by moving into the best position to take them and by doing this early. This is what footwork really is, at least from an advanced player's viewpoint.

If, without underestimating our opponents in the slightest, we realize the comparative easiness of most of the shots we receive from players of about our own standard, it is not being overconfident or swollen-headed to come to **expect most returns to go back into the court. In this** way alone—without doing anything about our own stroking— our control will improve.

I admit this sounds rather like a trick in which something is supposed to be made out of nothing. But it is a tennis fact. What it means is that you can make a start at increasing your control merely out of realization.

The role of racket-hand fingers

Another thing to remember about controlling the ball is that you have decidedly more feel in your fingers than you have in the palm of your hand. You cannot hold a racket handle completely in your fingers because it is too big; nor should you want to because you need the comfortable support of your palm. You can, however, get a feeling of having your fingers involved in the operation as distinct from heaving the ball over the net mainly from the weight of the butt of your hand.

It is true that in driving you can use the palm of your hand only and get away with it to a certain extent. You have the whole swing of your arm to provide a reasonable amount of speed, and the aspect of touch is often not very demanding. Nevertheless, with any drive that really calls for control, such as making an accurate passing shot or returning a most awkward service, you can't beat using your fingers.

With most volleys touch is essential. Imagine that a fast drive comes at you which you have to volley from close to the net and below it. Your fingers can absorb the pace of the ball. If you hold the racket right down in your palm you will find that if you get the ball over the net only the back fence will stop it.

Apart from the matter of touch, your fingers are stronger than you may have realized. You use them for throwing quite heavy objects. The normal service action is the equivalent of a throw, so that serving with the racket handle towards your fingers should seem the natural thing to do.

Lastly, when you hold a racket handle down in your palm it feels thicker than when it is in your fingers. When you first go on to play it sometimes feels a little thick, and if you haven't played for a long time the saying is that it feels like a mattock handle or the handle of a pick ax. By contrast, at the end of an afternoon's play, when you have your eye well in and are feeling completely relaxed, the handle seems smaller and more comfortable. The explanation of this can only be that while you are feeling somewhat strange you grasp the racket too much in your palm and that as your confidence grows you unconsciously tend to use your fingers more.

All this seems to indicate that the tennis gods intended us to use our fingers in holding the racket.

Feel and the weight of the ball

Feeling the ball confidently does not mean feeling *for* the ball or playing tentatively.

There are two main divisions of thought about it. Some people say that when playing their best they scarcely feel the weight of the ball. They sweep sweetly, the ball is taken plumb in the middle of the strings and is swept away with the racket head. The only time the ball seems to have any weight is when it fails to hit the middle and so jars. That is one way of feeling the ball. And feel it you must, because there's not much use in just hitting it.

There are a few things against this concept, however. It is likely to be too airy, and I doubt if you can count on it all the time. For instance, you are not likely to have it on windy days, it may not be there when anything upsets your rhythm, and somehow it does not seem to be suitable for playing game points or when you are scrambling.

The other school of thought is that you should feel the ball as a solid weight and hit against it. By this concept you feel the ball at its heaviest and most solid when it meets the center of your strings. When it hits anywhere off-center it feels lighter because the satisfying thump is missing.

Of the two methods, I think the second is by far the sounder. It's one that can always be with you, through thick and thin. It is most positive, because you need to feel the weight of the ball, and you will know without doubt on every shot you hit whether you *have* felt it or not. There are no half measures about that.

Long contact

This is so much akin to feeling the ball that the two either merge into one or are really the same thing expressed in different ways. For the sake of simplicity we will consider long contact with the forehand drive only.

In the hope that one of them will strike the right chord with you, here are some concepts of what is meant by long contact. Think of holding the ball on the strings as long as you possibly can before letting it go, like slinging a ball out of a lacrosse bat. Imagine the ball is made of putty and stays on your strings as you direct it instead of flying off before you are quite ready. Carry the ball along with your racket head. Go with the ball as far as you can. Hit straight through the ball as though your racket head were going to land in the spot where you want to send the ball.

The last sentence should have given you a clearer understanding of the follow-through, if by any chance you used to think (as I once did) that following through merely meant finishing with the racket somewhere out in front of you. Whenever you end a stroke with your racket in the correct position the ball has usually been hit well, but the real meaning of the term stands as following *through* the ball.

If you meet the ball squarely and go straight through it, it flattens out more and it actually does stay in contact with your strings a little longer. I am fairly sure, however, that this fraction of a second makes less difference to where your shots go than does your mental feeling of having stayed on the ball for an appreciable time as you controlled it on its way.

You need to convince yourself of the control you can get from long contact. As good a way as any is to practice drives against a friend, holding the ball on the strings in the most exaggerated manner possible. Hit longer and ıonger and heavier and heavier, and you should eventually get the feeling that unless you hit the ball far too high it will never go out. If you finally get the grand feeling that tennis courts have, after all, been designed to just the right length to hit the ball into instead of, as you formerly suspected, being purposely made about a foot or so too short—well, yours will be the earth and all that's in it.

Which part of the ball surface to hit

Now for the ball itself. You normally aim for the center of your strings, but by no means should you always hit the center of the ball. These off-center places are of course not marked on the ball. You have to find them for yourself, rather like a violinist making his own notes on the plain fingerboard of a violin.

When you want to do a sliced-service ace into the first court, serving wide of your opponent's forehand (and particularly if a strong diagonal wind is aiding you), don't you feel that you hit the upper right-hand part of the ball rather than its center? When you play against a man who hits a lot of short cross-court forehands for winners, doesn't he seem to be hitting the outside of the ball?

Here is a shot you may not have thought about, judging by the few times I see it attempted by players good enough to perform it:

Your opponent plays a shot, say to your backhand side, that is wide enough to send you beyond the sideline; he

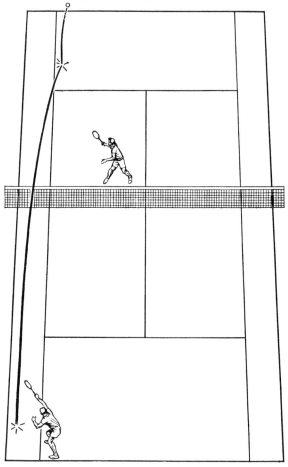

A DOWN-THE-LINE PASSING SHOT CURVING INWARDS
Hit outside the ball, as for a crosscourt shot, and the ball can pass beyond the net-player's reach and curve back inside the line.

follows in to the net, and you decide to go for a passing shot down the line. If you hit straight at the center of the ball, the odds are that your opponent will be able to reach it and cut it off or that as well as being out of his reach it will go out down the sidelines. Surely the way to hit it is on the outside of the ball, aiming it outside the sideline so that it has every chance of being out of reach while at the same time it is always angling inwards the farther it goes. You may think this is difficult to do. If you are really being forced, any shot is difficult, but in most circumstances it is the safest way to attempt this kind of shot.

Other specific instances will come to mind. In general, you should be fully conscious that although you use the center of the your strings to send the ball where you want it to go, you also use whatever part of the ball's surface happens to suit your purpose best.

Any discussion of hitting the ball anywhere other than at its center leads to a consideration of *spin*. It cannot be denied that spin is a wonderful means of ball control. You slice under a very low ball to lift it, and you slice round it to swerve it. You topspin high balls and those you wish to dip or angle sharply, and you use a kind of dragging topspin on awkward ones that might otherwise fly out of control. Nevertheless you would be most ill-advised to rely on spin as your only means of ball control. You would be almost certain to overdo it. Spin is discussed in some detail in following chapters dealing with grips and strokes.

The constant error in timing

Besides giving you more speed for less physical effort, *good timing* is a great asset to ball control. Many players do not give individual attention to their timing, regarding errors in it as part of their normal stroking. Timing errors can be isolated, however, and a definite attempt made to rectify them.

The error in timing is fairly constant; hence you can improve your timing as soon as you know what this error is. It is mostly that you hit too early.

An annoying thought, that. Here we all are, trying to be as alert as possible, using quick footwork, dutifully making early stroke preparation, and even anticipating and moving before our opponent hits some of his shots—and now we hear that most of our timing errors are caused by being too early. It is true, however, and the sooner we accept it by understanding why, the better off we shall be.

For a start, take timing in smashing a lob. Mistakes here are nearly always made by hitting too early and sending the ball into the net. In the extreme case of mistiming (where the player misses the ball altogether) the shot is invariably made before the ball comes down, never after it has passed.

Similarly with a drive. About the only time anyone is late with his timing and sends the ball out to his off-side is when he is forced into doing so. On the other hand, players continually hit too early at the ball and only prevent themselves from pulling these shots out across court by pushing their wrist forward in compensation.

Players will probably accept these practical examples as correct enough. Nevertheless it must seem strange indeed that thousands of normally accurate people do their level best to time a ball correctly and yet have a common error of being early. Here is the explanation. We time the ball in accordance with the general speed of our swing. Just before contact with the ball the racket head is traveling at its fastest—faster than at any other part of the swing. Apparently it is not normal for us to take this extra speed for a short distance into consideration. Hence the racket head tends to arrive early.

The timing pause

You may wish to return to practicalities and ask if there is any accepted method for preventing yourself from being too early. Some players count "one-two" as they pause and hit; some, more descriptively, mutter "pause-hit". I have even heard of "wait-weight"; so do not feel too odd if you have some similar pendulum-like formula of your own. Other players deliberately pause at the top of their backswing; others again (the majority) are merely conscious of the fact that their forward swing has to be delayed a fraction of a second.

Players who do not know that timing involves delaying the stroke a little, tend to sweep at the ball with backswing and forward swing combined in one motion. When they manage to do this smoothly they have some wonderful on-days. Some but all too few. A few gifted players apparently make no delay and yet consistently time the ball well. I can only repeat that they are a few gifted players.*

Mention of gifted players may call to mind some rising-ball experts you know. You may wonder whether they have their good timing merely because they take the ball earlier and so do not have to wait that fraction of the second needed to counteract the natural tendency to be too early. The answer is most definitely no. A rising ball is the hardest one to time correctly, and in doing so you still need to have your fractional delay. The easiest place to time the ball is where it is at its slowest, which is just after the top of its bounce.

Probably the most important factor in being master of your own fate in timing the ball is early preparation for the stroke. Then you have only to time the forward sweep of it.

I should emphasize that the pause before sweeping forward is not necessarily a dead stop in your swing. It can be a slight slowing-down near the top of it. Against a fast ball it could perhaps be even more mental than actual. But in most cases it should be there. Without that fractional pause your timing of a few shots here and there may happen to be right, but it is more likely to be too early.

* In intentionally swinging smoothly and continuously throughout the whole swing the concept is that power is automatically built into the stroke, so that any pressing is eliminated and the forward swing can be entirely devoted to controlling the ball. This can work sweetly when you are practicing, but you need natural timing and mental calmness to rely on it in a close match. I assume it is for artists only; but try it—in this particular aspect you might be an artist.

CHAPTER THREE

Getting to grips with your opponent's game

*Grips/Styles of play/Tactics against strengths
and weaknesses*

As an advanced player, you are probably not concerned with altering your already settled and natural grip. In this chapter, therefore, we will look at our opponents' games—and in doing so we can expect to learn a few points about our own as well.

The way in which a man holds his racket influences his whole style of play. This resulting style of play—with experience, seen even in the warm-up—is usually accompanied by characteristic strengths and weaknesses. If you know what these styles of play are, you will not need to play a man several times before you know which parts of his game to exploit and which to be wary of.

Standard grips

The three standard forehand grips are probably well known to you already. They are usually described by the position of the V made by the thumb and forefinger on the handle of a racket held straight out in front of you with the short strings pointing up and down. In the Western grip, the V lies somewhere on the right bevel of the handle and points in the general direction of the right shoulder. With Eastern grips the V lies in the center of the top surface of the handle or slightly to the right of it and points a little to the right of the center of your body. With Continental grips, the V lies anywhere from left of center of the top surface to somewhere on the left bevel.

GRIPS

WESTERN FOREHAND:

V on right bevel. Palm towards bottom surface. Wrist well behind handle. Middle, third, and little fingers reach so far round front surface that their middle knuckles face forward in direction of shot.

EASTERN FOREHAND:

V to right of center of top surface. Palm and large knuckle of index finger on rear surface. Middle, third, and index fingers well up front surface.

EASTERN FOREHAND:

V in center of top surface. Palm and large knuckle of index finger on rear surface.

CONTINENTAL:

V near ridge between top surface and left bevel. Palm towards top surface. Large knuckle of index finger somewhere on right bevel or on its lower ridge.

FULL CONTINENTAL:

V in center of left bevel. Palm above top surface. Large knuckle of index finger on right bevel.

The position of the palm may give a more practical means of description.

The Western grip is the one naturally taken on a carpet-beater in hitting a rug hanging from a clothesline. Using it on a tennis racket means that, for the strings to be square-on to the ball, the palm of the hand is mainly under the handle. Assuming as always that the body is sideways to the net, the ball would have to be met well out in front of the left hip. The backhand grip is obtained by turning the racket head over the top and adjusting a little to open the face of the racket; the same face of the racket is used to hit the ball, which has to be met well in front of the right hip.

When two people shake hands, the grip that each has on the other's hand is the *Eastern grip*. On a racket the palm is mainly behind the handle and the ball is met about opposite the left hip. For the backhand grip the palm is turned towards the top of the handle and the thumb advanced diagonally across the back; the ball is met a little in front of the right hip.

In hammering down a nail on a bench you would be using the *Continental forehand grip*, unless you happen to have extended your thumb along one side of the handle; with a racket the thumb goes round the handle for strength of grip. The palm is more on top of the handle than it is in the Eastern grip, and the ball is met just behind the left hip. The Continental backhand grip is virtually the same, the thumb remaining wrapped round the handle for strength of grip, or else advanced diagonally for support; in either case the ball is played from a little in front of the right hip.

Apart from the diagonal thumb position, there is little difference between the full Continental forehand and its backhand and the Eastern backhand. In practice, though, many Continental-type players play the forehand with the palm somewhat less to the top of the handle and make a very small change for the backhand.

So much for the mechanics of grips, which, after all, everyone seems to explain somewhat differently in points of detail. It is now time to look at the styles of play that result from them. Naturally, we shall have to be somewhat critical of all of them.

Opposing "Western Style" tennis

We will follow normal procedure and discuss (and largely discount) the Western style first of all. Though still supported in the Western states of America (through a combination of concrete courts and high-bouncing balls), it has long been on the decline in Australia. It is essentially a rugged style, its exponents often using an almost tearing topspin on their shots. This makes them severe on short high balls and also enables them to get a lot of angle without missing the sidelines.

The disadvantages of the Western grip are that it is fairly docile against low balls, weak against wide ones, and for those that get behind the player, hopeless; in short, it cannot compare with the flexibility of the Eastern and Continental grips. Nevertheless a Western-type player always makes an awkward antagonist, as his unusual shots tend to make his opponents stroke below their usual form.

From the above, your tactics will be obvious. Do not set up short high balls for your opponent to attack, and do not come in to the net on any shot he can get a really good hit at. Keep the ball low and wide as much as possible. Always try to entice him in a little so that you can get your next shot somewhat behind him, and then follow it to the net; look for such an opportunity after his return of service. Try not to be upset by his kicking topspin bounces. Keep going; the Western style is tiring for its user, no matter how fiery he may be in the first set.

Various Eastern styles

The Eastern grip is used by so many people and spoken of so much that it has come to be regarded as the only grip worth using. Be that as it may, it does not help you with your recognition of types and their attendant strengths and weaknesses. It is important to realize from the start that distinct types do exist among Eastern players, because the actual grips they use vary so much. The name itself is fashionable, so that forehand grips more Continental than Eastern, and those right round the handle to being almost Western, tend to be included in it.

We need to break up this all-embracing Eastern grip into its main groups and see what styles of play result.

With most volleys touch is essential.
Laver's fingers absorb the pace of the ball.
(See text, pages 28–29)

Roy Emerson lashes on plenty of topspin
to hit himself out of an awkward position.
(See text, page 33)

Standard Eastern. The V down the center of the top surface of the racket handle, and straight strokes, flat or slightly rolled, with the forehand (played from near the left hip) probably stronger (but not lopsidedly so) than the backhand (played from a little in front of the right hip). The strength of this game is its soundness, with no apparent weakness anywhere. An opponent using this style is always a good player, and with such orthodox strokes he deserves to be. However, there has to be a weakness somewhere, or else this player would not be in the same grade as we are. His weakness, for want of a better word, is that he may have no great power anywhere. Although you cannot take liberties and come to the net on anything short against such an accurate type, when you do come in on good ones you are not likely to run into any fireworks. Also, you yourself usually play better against this straight type of player than against any other. None of his shots are vicious, and there is always a noticeable lack of strain in playing a game where you can play the ball anywhere without having to concentrate on keeping it away from some dangerous stroke.

Next comes a modification of this type, the *long-swinging Standard Eastern.* These players have more power and are the ones who specialize in deep drives from both forehand and backhand. If one of them is of about the same standard as a player in the previous group, the longer-swinging man is almost certain to be less good on short balls and at the net.

With both these types you should try to break up the rallies by changing both pace and length. Orthodox players sometimes rely too heavily on their stroking alone and are reluctant to scramble for their points.

Eastern towards Western Styles. This is the group using a grip farther round behind the handle—that is, towards the Western. Their basic characteristic is a long and powerful rolled forehand, hit from farther in front of the left hip. Their most probable weaknesses (as with the Western, as you would expect) are in handling low and wide balls and those that get behind the player. This group now subdivides into two, decided by how the backhand is played. First come the conscientious characters who undertake a large change of grip in order to have a backhand to match their forehand. They often achieve this, but then suffer a weakness which falls literally between forehand and backhand—in the form of vulnerability against any fast low ball played straight at them, particularly when they are at the net.

The second subdivision is the more usual one. In this the players make only a small change for the backhand, and, as this change was started from a forehand grip farther round than the orthodox Eastern, it follows that the backhand grip in its turn is not really far enough round for the stroke to be strong. In fact it is weak, usually a short cut—as distinct from a long and strong downward slice—and it can be attacked and followed to the net with little risk of meeting sustained passing shots. The players in this subdivision are almost always lopsided in strength. It is interesting to note that their stroke production is actually lopsided, too, in that they play their big forehands well in front of their bodies and their retiring backhands farther back beside them. By "lopsided" I do not mean that these players are necessarily ungraceful. They can well have smooth, powerful forehands and small, neat-looking backhands. I merely mean that there are large differences between forehand and backhand both in strength and in where they take the ball in relation to the body.

You can see that I am trying to be polite to everyone, but now I have to refer to something that definitely is awkward and ungainly. Included in this present subdivision of players who use an inadequate backhand grip are those who, in spite of having this grip, still take the ball in front of the right hip. This means that the wrist is ahead of the racket and the arm bowed, and this backhand stroke is about as weak as it can be.

In playing against any player of the strong-forehand/ weak-backhand type the backhand is obviously the target, but it can be the most elusive target you ever tried to find. These players are usually very fast about the court and can make a forehand out of almost everything you send over.

Often the best forehand that most of them have is played from a ball directed well towards their backhand, when they get round it and either pull a clean winner straight down the line wide of your own forehand or else slide it to the off at a sharp angle away from your backhand.

To stop these players' forehands from dominating the whole game you have to find their backhands. You do this by playing first to the forehand with a shot that is good enough to prevent their immediately taking charge of the exchange and that forces them to leave their backhand side open to your next stroke. With great preference towards a flat rising-ball shot (if you are safe enough with these), you then pierce mercilessly into that exposed and weak backhand and follow in.

If you are not good enough with your preparatory shot to this type of player's forehand you will never get at his backhand. It is strange but true, when you are opposed to a good player of the *strong-forehand type,* that although his weak backhand is both his worry and your constant objective, the one shot you need more than any other is a penetrating cross-court forehand drive of your own to force him to expose his backhand.

These players can be very dangerous opponents, particularly in a final set. It goes to show than no one with a very strong forehand is ever easily beaten.

Playing a left-hander

Last among the Easterners is the left-hander. Left-handers vary less than right-handers, most being like the unbalanced type of right-hander already described. Often they are more exaggerated, the forehand being stronger again and the backhand even more suspect. In singles they delight in forehand passing shots that leave you stranded. In doubles their forehands can carry such dip and control as to make you wonder why you ever bothered to learn any shot other than a backhand half-volley.

For the backhand this kind of left-hander reluctantly

changes grip by about the same small amount as his unbalanced right-handed cousin. The reason his stroke is often even weaker is that in order to reach a right-hander's backhand the left-hander has to play to his off-side. In doing so he tends to lift his elbow and drop the head of his racket. This becomes his natural way of making a backhand stroke and results in turn in his usually having the poorest cross-court backhand passing shot of any type of player you will meet. By cross-court here I mean wide of the right-hander's forehand volley.

The apparent reason the average left-hander develops in this way is that from early youth he has always played in the left or second court in doubles. Taking nearly every serve on his forehand, he uses the grip (Eastern modified farther round behind the handle, towards Western) that is probably the most effective of the lot—provided forehand returns of service were the only strokes that ever had to be played. On the odd occasion in his early days when he has had to play a backhand (and from a very tender age he has been a past master at avoiding them) he has found his natural backhand going straight to the opposing net man. To keep clear of this obstacle he steers the ball away to his off with raised elbow and dropped racket head.

But do not bother to feel sorry for the left-hander. Besides helping him to develop the most effective doubles forehand that exists, nature has given him the opportunity of having a great advantage in service, so it is only fair if his backhand brings him back to the level of his friends. Not right back, however. With about even strokes, a left-hander has an inbuilt advantage over a right-hander; in other words, the right-hander usually needs to have clearly superior strokes in order to beat him.

Once play reaches a standard where the right-handers have sufficient accuracy to get at their left-handed opponents' backhands, this weakness becomes too big a load to carry. Somewhere at about this stage the left-hander becomes less of a threat in singles and is feared far more as a doubles opponent.

Manuel Santana is Spanish, but his grip is "All-American."
This one is Eastern-towards-Western.
(See text, page 43)

Charles Pasarell comes from Puerto Rico, but this grip is Continental. (See text, page 50)

Many people say they feel awkward when playing left-handers and admit that they don't know why. The reason is that a left-hander is usually better equipped to attack a right-hander's backhand than a right-hander is to attack a left-hander's. A left-hander can swing his serve to the backhand in either court, his natural forehand is across court, and his natural backhand is to his off-side. Conversely, the normal right-hander's service is not accurate in delivering center-line serves into the second court, and he usually prefers straight forehands and crosscourt backhands; playing down-the-line backhands, particularly, he feels weak.

If you get this trussed-up feeling against a left-handed opponent and are slowly losing ground as the match progresses, you may as well take your courage in both hands and adopt the tactics given a moment ago for playing unbalanced right-handers: play wide to the forehand, then to the exposed backhand, and go in to the net.

Tactically, it is easier to serve to a left-hander than to a right-hander. He makes you a present of his backhand in the first court, while in the second you can serve wide of his forehand, return to his backhand, and come in. For both courts you are using your long diagonal serve to the corners —the easiest one to hit into court.

Unless you have an accurate center-line serve to the second court, or unless the left-hander leaves a fair-sized gap, it is better not to try to attack his backhand. You are likely to miss a lot of first services, and your second may not be accurate enough to prevent him from stepping round it and producing one of those unpredictable forehands of his that leave you standing.

The left-handed type I have described will probably decrease in numbers in the future. With the model set for them by Rod Laver, we can expect to see a crop of balanced left-handed players develop. In the meantime, of course, no one reading this should think that all present-day left-handers are like my so-called typical left-hander. I use him as a definite identity in my range of types. Other left-handers may fit into any of the balanced right-handed types described—

so well, in fact, that except on service their left-handedness loses much of its significance. This includes the Continental style(which follows below) where a left-hander can be a particularly attractive stroke-maker, in the manner of Laver and Tony Roche.

Combating Continental styles

The Continental can be a grip of extremes. It seems to develop a forehand that is either very good or else not as good as the player's own backhand. This applies particularly to the full Continental, where the thumb and forefinger V is well over on the left bevel and the palm is so much towards the top of the racket handle that the forehand and backhand grips are identical. Because of this possibly weak forehand, the Continental has received justified criticism.

Weaker forehand. This type of player's ground-strokes are really based on the backhand, but we may not notice it because the backhand shot is not powerfully made. It is usually flexible, playing balls well that are wide, low, behind the player, on the rise, etc. It is neat and effective (you find, eventually), but it is not an obvious type of backhand strength.

The forehand is good on low and wide balls and is often steady enough to rally all day, but it falls down against a net attack. The usual basic flaw that causes this failure is that the wrist is held too stiffly. Coupled with a downward action on the forward swing, this inevitably results in the stroke having underspin. The player himself may not even know it and may think that he is hitting flat. This does not really matter. It is the underspin itself that counts—to your advantage. It greatly reduces the speed any shot can have and yet stay in court, and with attempted cross-court passing shots it usually means that the ball goes within reach of the net man's forehand volley or out over the sideline.

Once you recognize this type of player, your tactics should be to attack his forehand and come to the net, knowing that the down-the-line passing shot or the lob will be his usual answers.

Supporters of the Continental style of play claim that this underspin stroke should not really be called a Continental forehand at all as it is only the other side (and a pale image, too) of the player's backhand. I must say that I agree with the last part of this. I have noticed that a lot of these players hold their thumb diagonally across the racket handle and really do look as if they are hitting a forehand with a backhand grip. However, though these players may not represent the Continental grip at its best, they do exist and you should recognize them and know how to play them. Otherwise you can be in for trouble. They are mostly steady from the baseline and deft at the net, so they are far from being pushovers.

Stronger forehand. In passing now to the true Continental exponents you might like to leave our discussion of players of our own standard for a few moments and take a look at some champions.

Though we often read of the Eastern grip in association with famous players, it has always seemed to me that the Continental-type champion is seldom acknowledged to be using a Continental grip in any form. Instead we hear him referred to as having exceptionally graceful and flexible strokes (Jack Crawford), as being probably the best forehand of his day (Drobny), as being so powerful that he can play "wristy" strokes safely (Lew Hoad), or as having a style that is a left-handed version of Hoad's (Rod Laver).

It seems it was ever thus. The style of play of the great French master of the 1920's, Henri Cochet, used to be described in all sorts of superlatives, but, Continental though it was, I cannot remember ever reading this description of it. The Continental grip was probably used by many, if not most, of the early Wimbledon champions, including the immortal Doherty brothers; the Continental was once called the English grip, and, as we know, the game of lawn tennis started in England.

The one famous Continental player — a three-times Wimbledon winner—whose name was often linked with this grip was Fred Perry. Perhaps this was because his grip was a more extreme example of the Continental than that used by some of the others I have named. Perhaps I am alone in regarding all the others as Continental players. Perhaps some of them do not even regard themselves as such, and might by annoyed by this classification.

Well, they should know their own games best, of course, but this is the way it appears to me.

Though all the players whose names I have used would not have had the same grip (any more than any given group of Eastern players would have), they all had more similarity to each other in style than any one of them had to an Eastern player.

Difference between Eastern and Continental styles

The basic points of the Eastern grip are that the wrist is solidly behind the handle, the palm of the hand is behind it, and the large knuckle of the index finger rests somewhere on the rear surface of the racket handle. Being essentially behind the ball, the style looks strong and straight-ahead. The basic points of the Continental grip are that the wrist and palm are more towards the top of the handle with the index knuckle resting somewhere on the right bevel of the handle (that is, the angled surface between its top and rear surfaces). With this grip, forehand and backhand seem to be more closely allied, and the play, even with a powerful hitter, looks more dextrous—somewhat akin to giant-sized table tennis.

Taken as a group, the players I have named were all stylists. They were rising-ball experts, free-wristed and so flexible that they seemed to play all shots—high, low, behind them, wide, or off their shoelaces—with equal ease. All sent the ball back very fast, whether from timing or from power.

Last, and most important, they were all stronger on the forehand than on the backhand. To me this seems a strong argument that the Continental forehand grip is not outdated and of academic interest only.

No American champions in the list? There is a reason. The Americans developed the Eastern American and Western

American grips (to give them their full names), so presumably they began with the English/Continental. Pictures of some of their very early champions indicate this. Leaving aside the golden West with its concrete surfaces and high bounces, the reason the Americans have completely adopted the American grips in either form stems from the hardness of the balls they use.

The compression of tennis balls should be within internationally approved tolerances, so U.S. balls may be made from slightly different materials than those used in the balls of other countries. At all events, to an Australian they seem as hard as golf balls and shoot off your racket and over the baseline until you carefully adjust to them. All this indicates that American conditions call for a wrist behind the racket, a closed racket face, and a determination to keep the ball down at all costs. Allowing for a possible exception in Gonzales, America is therefore no breeding-ground for the Continental grip, at any rate in its more extreme form.

Returning from the stars to solid earth, we do not find many *full-Continental strong-forehand* players about. I don't know whether this is because the grip has been discredited (certainly it is never taught) or because you have to be something of a tennis genius to begin with before you can have a good forehand with a full Continental grip. Probably it is because it puts too much strain on the average wrist to be successfully used. However, we do meet plenty of those Continental players who use a forehand grip nearer to the Eastern and who make a small change for the backhand. Even if their grip is called Eastern at times or "something between Continental and Eastern" at others, the thing that concerns us to their opponents is that they have Continental-style characteristics.*

* Perhaps I am inviting argument here by calling such a grip Continental and not Modified-Eastern. I have done so because once the palm of the hand is no longer completely and solidly behind the handle the resulting style of play tends to differ from the Eastern styles described in the previous Eastern section. Perhaps one day this might come to be known as the Australian grip. Everyone, including the purest of the purists, might then be satisfied.

Tactics against strong forehand Continentals

If any type of free-stroking Continental opponent is in our class, he certainly must have his weaknesses. Therefore we should not be too overawed in the warm-up if he plays all shots with apparent ease. Weaknesses will show up in the match.

The man he most resembles is the very first one I described, the orthodox Eastern, but he is likely to be less sound because the Eastern grip is basically sounder. So your pointers to weaknesses are that he may not have any particular power anywhere, and, because of possible unsoundness, that he is likely to make his share of mistakes.

Keep the ball in play and, in baseline exchanges, quite high over the net if you like. Possibly in the middle of a rally he will take a ball well on the rise that he need not have, and miss it; and with any lack of concentration on his part, his easy style of play can become mere mildness.

Do not be too surprised or discouraged if you come to the net behind a very good shot and are passed with apparent ease. These players can pull a lot out of the bag without any of it looking fluky; just remember that they tend to make quite a few mistakes, too. When they in their turn come to the net, again do not be too dismayed if they volley and half-volley your lowest shots with confidence and because of this ability can afford to volley from farther back from the net, meaning that they can also cover lobs very well. In compensation, if some of your passing shots get a little too high they may not be disposed of in one volley, giving you a second chance. Continental players tend to overdo it and stand a little too far back from the net, giving you more chance with a cross-court passing shot than other players do.

Finally, beware of letting yourself get discouraged. If one of these players is leading you on games and has been handling everything you send him with that characteristic ease, then more than against any other type of player you are likely to get the deflating feeling that he could beat you with his overcoat on. A good Continental player, always a delight to onlookers, can make you feel you are engaged in a hare and tortoise race. If the latter role fits you, do not give up; keep on the job and hope he will relapse into the equivalent of a short sleep every now and again. If you are a good Eastern player in your own right, then let him have his brilliant rapier—you have your stronger sword.

Strategy against backhand strength players

You must recognize stronger-backhand players at once. You can, too—so easily that perhaps you will think I am insulting your intelligence by suggesting that you may not. Once again it is amazing how many people are reluctant to believe the evidence of their own eyes, and lose by playing throughout a match to what is actually the other man's strength.

The *Continental stronger-backhand* type passes unnoticed as often as not. Experienced players of this kind actually conceal their backhand strength, winning points from this side with the least possible display of having any preference for it. Nevertheless, from what has been explained in the preceding Continental section you should now be able to recognize these players and play your own game accordingly.

The other group of backhand players—who bat, golf, or chop wood left-handed and are clearly more at home whenever their right side is forward—are obvious to anyone. These players mostly have a *powerful backhand* made from a grip well behind the handle and usually with the thumb straight up the back. Normally they don't attempt a forehand drive, but substitute that small type of cut mentioned earlier as being safe but weak against net play. You should attack the forehand cut and take the net, and when playing to your opponent's strong but non-flexible backhand try to get the ball behind it.

You may wonder why any type of underspin forehand is always described as being weak against net play when so many good players have a sliced backhand and seem to get along all right with it. It's like this. Although most

55

people can hit harder on the forehand side when driving, the forehand slice cannot normally be made as strongly as the backhand can. Drives are swinging strokes, and a longer swing is possible on the forehand side. Slices, etc., are short strokes, where any small extra length of swing on the forehand side scarcely applies; instead it is the wrist that counts, and you can get more purchase or leverage with a backhand action. Naturally there are exceptions, but in most cases the player with a flat or slightly rolled forehand and a sliced backhand is more evenly balanced than the man with a big backhand and a forehand cut.

Against freak grips and styles

You need to be able to sort these out to avoid feeling confused when you meet one of them.

Most double-handed players serve and play the forehand right-handed and use two hands for the backhand. This two-handed backhand is usually the stronger side and always the steadier. Never waste your energy banging your first serve straight into this backhand—it is rocklike. Its weakness is that it lacks reach, so you would normally play to this man's forehand and then wide of his backhand, or vice-versa. Because he always plays in the second court in doubles his preferences for direction are down-the-line for forehand and cross-court for backhand. When playing to his forehand and taking the net, guard against the straight forehand and the toss.

When the double-hander uses two hands for his forehand he is putting all his eggs in one basket by becoming most lopsided in strength. On his left side he will have to play his backhand using only half the handle's length, or else he must use his weaker left arm as a forehand. Similarly, a man who uses two hands for both forehand and backhand has his strong and weak sides, the strong side being where the grip is natural (as in swinging a baseball bat) and the weak one where his hands are the wrong way round (because he

Ion Tiriac's forehand is not always well-produced—
but, like everything about him, it is effective.
(See text, page 87)

Cliff Richey's firm-wristed forehand (see text, page 88).
The left foot is a fraction late,
but this shot will be placed across the front leg.
(See text, page 115)

hasn't got time to change). He has the added weakness of lack of reach on both sides.

Ambidextrous players are usually right-handed servers with a stronger forehand on the right side than on the left. Often the left-handed forehand is somewhat hooked and has a strong preference for cross-court direction. These players have maximum reach on both sides but dislike balls played straight at them—particularly on the volley, where they sometimes have no shot at all.

These are the general types from which to chart your course; but freaks will be freaks. I once played a naturally right-handed man with a strong right-handed forehand, a secondary left-handed forehand and a swinging *left*-handed service. Invulnerable to an opponent's service, he could swing his own left-handed serve onto the opposing backhand. But he did not have the advantage in every way. Fortunately he happened to be too fat, and two weaknesses resulted: he had to carry himself after the wide ones, and he could not get himself out of the way of those hit straight at him.*

And champions will be champions. They exploit to the full the strength and solidity of the two-handed grip, and overcome inherent weaknesses on the other side. Look at Pancho Segura, for instance. His two-handed forehand vies with the great forehands of Crawford and Perry as one of the best all-purpose strokes in the history of the game, and then he manages to obtain a full-handle length grip for his backhand by a bewilderingly swift changing of hands.

If you are a member of this club, do not discard any good shot you have. Keep on sending it over harder and harder at those one-armed commoners.

* A test in sorting things out. A right-handed man plays his two-handed backhand with his hands the wrong way round (that is, with his left hand at the bottom of the racket handle); he plays his forehand right-handed at half-handle length.

Q. What is his inherent weakness, and how should you play?

A. Reach. Try playing wide to both sides, in the hit-up.

In general: Any freak shot is usually strong in itself—otherwise its owner would not persist in playing it in a freak manner.

Many players anticipate the strengths and weaknesses of various opponents purely by instinct. Not being able to explain such an intangible, I have chosen grips and resulting styles as the basis of my analysis. Some readers will have assimilated it all; others will at least have recognized their own games and should now have a better idea of the tactics an opponent is likely to use against them.

Most will understand that recognizing natural strengths and weaknesses can make the difference between winning and losing against anyone of your own standard; while it cannot mean beating all the better players, it certainly cuts them down nearer to size. But does any of it interfere with watching the ball—consciously and for the whole of its flight? Not in the slightest.

A few may feel they are not up to it yet and in the meantime would prefer to concentrate entirely on their own play. I know that some younger players find anything other than their own strokes more distracting than helpful. Again you must please yourself, as you are the one who plays your matches. But have no doubt about this: whether you read your opponents' games or not, consciously or instinctively an experienced player of any age always reads yours.

CHAPTER FOUR

Training your big guns

Attacking service / Solid overhead

Here is a yardstick that anyone, whatever his standard of play, can apply to his own service. A serve is positive if you try to do something with it; it is neutral if you merely put it into play; it is shaky if the main hope behind it is to avoid a double-fault.

Positive serves aim for aces, for getting back the type of shot you are set up for, or for preventing your opponent from giving you a dangerous shot. They comprise any or a combination of the following factors: speed, angle (either going sharply away from the receiver or coming in towards his body), depth towards the service line, direction to the weaker side, and awkward bounce.

Neutral serves abound in social tennis and in practice sets. In matches they occur when a player loses concentration or eases up because the match is well in hand.

Shaky serves are the bugbear of most of us. If the term applies to our first serve as well as to our second, they are a nightmare.

The ideal is to send over a positive serve at will. If we haven't enough confidence to serve this way at least most of the time, we need to find out why.

As always, the first thing to do is to look for a constant error. One does exist. With all overhead strokes it is hitting the ball down into the net. Next time you watch a game see for yourself how many first serves are banged into the net (sometimes a string of three in succession)—and how many second serves are popped into it.

Some quite good players justify this to themselves by saying that they are not champions anyway and so have to expect a lot of misses. They claim they have to allow for hitting quite a few into the net because they have to aim low or else their serve tends to go out. That's wrong thinking, almost as bad as believing that to prevent your serve from going out you should stand a yard or two behind the baseline —and no self-respecting advanced player would dream of doing that.

Try it this way. You must aim the ball over the net. If you hit the middle of the strings (and especially if you happen to hit a fraction above the middle), then unless you hit the ball far too high over the net it will not go out. What can send it out, then? Hitting below the **center** of your strings. If you hit the ball down in this danger region even a half-pace serve tends to go up and out. Try it.

While we are on these two points of looking for a constant error and of hitting the **center** of the strings, if the racket often twists in your hand because you hit the ball near the side frame, I think you will find the mis-hit is practically always towards the outside or right-hand frame. Knowing this, you can correct your swing for it.

Avoiding double faults

Now we will concentrate on trying to remove the double fault bogey. There are a few aids to this, and perhaps you don't know about all of them.

When you serve a double fault that is not just bad luck but one that lowers your confidence, it is always good policy to serve the next first ball either in or at least as a definite sighter for the second. This isolates your double faults.

If you ever feel at all uncertain before a second serve, a good idea is to keep your back toe in contact with the ground until after you have hit the ball. This does have the accompanying disadvantage of reducing your power and delaying, though only fractionally, any advance to the net. But it means you are shooting from a steady platform, and it completely prevents that well-known kind of double fault where you fall forward and the ball goes only about halfway up the net.

THROWING THE BALL UP TO SERVE

A shorter throw is always a great aid to steadiness. Not necessarily a lower throw, but shorter in distance from your hand. Do not release the ball too low down, making a long throw of it. If you hold the ball near the tips of your fingers and thumb and throw your arm up to nearly its full height before letting the ball go (leaving your arm up there if you like), you will get the safe feeling of being able to set the ball up such a comparatively short distance away that you can hardly go wrong. But don't overdo it to an extent where you throw too low and therefore have to hurry your swing.

Your head should be kept in its place. Keep it up till you have hit the ball, or you will not be watching the ball at impact. This is not as natural as you may think. Dropping the head is done by a lot of people on Saturday afternoons, and by still more on Sunday afternoons, if you take my meaning.

A steady back foot, hand, and head are a great help in trying times. One such instance of trial that comes to mind is having a score of three-four, 30-40, one fault served, and a gust of wind comes along. Another is where there is some delay after your first serve but in the end you do not get two more. When these delays occur, always make sure of getting your second serve over the net, as most double-faults in these circumstances are served into the net, many of them striking the tape.

Lastly, it is good policy never to use more action than you need on any stroke, and this applies to second serves. You may see very good servers using as fast an action on their slower second serves as they do on their first ones; the reason is that they are applying a lot of spin and have to hit *at* the second ball just about as hard, even though they do not send it away as fast. If you are merely sending your second serve over more slowly than the first you should slow down your action or restrict the arc of your swing a little; you should always feel that you are putting pressure on the ball, not that you are drawing away from it.

Starting with a lot of service action and then drawing off the ball can give you a very weak feeling at the knees.

Clark Graebner's picture shows a lot of strength,
but this backhand grip is clearly inadequate.
(See text, page 93)

65

Rosemary Casals, with wrist held low and farther back than in Graebner's picture, adds firmness to a backhand.
(See text, page 93)

This is important, but once again don't overdo it or you will be pushing at the ball instead of hitting it.

The most common double-fault goes like this: first serve out, second into the net. The first serve is hit hard but below the center of the strings and out it goes, almost automatically. The server, unaware that this was the reason, carefully aims his second one lower; being careful, he hits the center of the strings, and this, together with his low aim, sends the ball into the net. To avoid this mistake hit the middle of the strings and aim over the net with the first and second services.

Compensating on off-days

We all have our off-days. Many players sometimes go further than that and experience what I can only call an unreal day, the service being the stroke mainly affected. You have more company than you may have imagined if this applies to you.

On these unreal days you have a constant service error. You know it is a constant error, but you just cannot seem to get over it. It might be that you cannot get any power, or that you hit every fast first serve out, or that you hit every fast first serve into the net.

If you cannot get any power, throw the ball higher, bend your elbow a lot more during your swing, turn sideways to the net, and do not turn before you have hit the ball. This should give you back all the power you ever had.

If your first serves all go out, you can ease off a little (only a little, or you will soon be shakily patting the ball), but you will already know from this chapter that the main remedy is to hit the center of the strings. Whether you are serving flat or sliced serves, remember to put the racket head a little over the ball as well. Serves, like drives, are long strokes, so make them with long contact on the strings.

If your fast first serves all go into the net, throw the ball higher. If that doesn't cure it, throw the ball a little farther back as well.

There is another method of compensating on days when your serve feels tight and will not go over the net or when it feels wild and flies away from you. The remedy is merely to open or close the racket face.

SERVICE
Toes in line with line of flight.

Stand sideways and hold your racket down beside your right leg. Now open the racket face a little by turning your hand and racket face slightly outwards to the right, or clockwise. Letting your racket head describe the largest arc that it can, you serve. This is the very opposite of feeling tight.

Hold your racket down by your right leg again. This time close the face a little. Lift your wrist up and serve, feeling that you are making a small arc with your wrist, as distinct from a large one with your racket head, and you should get a feeling of controlling the ball in a downward curve. This is the very opposite of feeling wild.

Somewhere between these two extremes you should find the serve that is comfortable, even on your most "unreal" days. Try it out on the court in practice and you will have an adjusting mechanism ready for a match.

"Unreal" days happen to experienced players just as they do to juniors. The difference in their effect is that the experienced players know how to make the right adjustment. You never hear them say there was nothing they could do about it. However, to play very badly all day (without being overmatched) is only inexperience; it is not poor temperament.

Overcoming foot-faults

Everyone foot-faults occasionally, and most players do it almost continuously. The nicest chap ever to set foot on a tennis court usually puts his foot on the backline as well. Foot-faulting irritates everyone who notices it, and it usually upsets the server if an umpire calls him. It somehow feels as though one were being accused of unfair play.

Officials have relaxed the rules to a point where all you can do wrong is to take a walking start or tread on the line. No one takes a long walk, but many take one long pace. It is the first step in a walk, and hence it is a walk. Anyone who is aware of this can stop it.

Treading on the line is the real trouble. If you have a highly energetic service action with lots of shuffling of feet and you carefully start off about half an inch behind the line it's time to stop deceiving yourself. You need a foot— and every inch of it, too, and for your second serve as well.

If you believe you serve from a steady front foot, it is still heavy odds that you actually do move this front foot by a couple of inches or so. The explanation is that although a steady server takes up what is a comfortable stance, he likes to have his feet still farther apart as he is hitting the ball—and so he shuffles his front one forward and foot-faults.

If he started with his feet wider apart he would not feel comfortable. So what is he to do? One of two things.

He can start about four inches behind the line. If he hates doing that—and most people do—he can take up his position with his front foot somewhat nearer the line, and just as he leans back to set himself for his serve he can move his back foot a little farther back. If this latter method fits in with your type of service action, I strongly recommend it to you.

We have everything to gain by making some little concession to the undoubted fact that we all tend to foot-fault. Make this concession *before* you start (that is, in your own time) and you will find that you are all clear to watch the ball and to put everything into your serve without ever thinking of a foot-fault in the middle of it or of being pulled up for one when you are halfway in to the net. It's well worth it.

Smashing: The key factors

The smash is the really big gun of tennis. The man playing it is always the dominating figure at the time. People who cannot smash well often envy those who can, but almost anyone can learn the art.

Contrary to general belief you do not need to have a powerful service upon which to build. Nor do you need to be either tall or strong. Since you usually have more time to position yourself, there is probably less need of height and reach in smashing than in any other stroke.

There are other misconceptions about smashing, caused perhaps by the very name of the stroke. In reality the main points are (a) timing, which amounts to being prepared to wait in a poised position for some time before finally hitting; (b) hitting the ball in the center of the strings; and (c) aiming it over the net—as with the service. Another important point, similar to the one already made about the second service, is that you should not use too much action.

Your smashing action will naturally resemble that of your service, but do not imagine that it has to be identical. In serving you need a fair amount of winding-up because you are right at the back of the court and have to accelerate a ball that is practically stationary. In smashing high lobs a lot of this winding-up is unnecessary; action should be kept to a minimum so that you will not build up complications and inaccuracies.

You do not need the downswing and complete loop behind the back, nor the bent knees, arched back, kicked racket head, or whatever else you employ to get power into your service. You are safer without them, stripped down to essentials. A short trial on the court will show that with far less action you can get just as much speed from a smash as you can from your normal serve. In brief: swing the racket round behind your back to serve; take it up in front of you to smash.

The basic action for smashing

Here is a suggested basic action for your smash against a high lob. Put your left hand up towards the ball. This is important because it makes you turn side-on and keeps you side-on for as long as possible, whereas many players seem to make an early right-sided fall or even a sort of collapse at the ball, usually disastrously. Leave your left arm up there as long as you like, comfortably. Bend your right elbow and hold your right hand cocked and ready by your right shoulder.

Stay poised in this manner until you judge the right moment; then, either keeping your back foot on the ground for steadiness or rising in the air to meet the ball, hit the back of the ball (not the top) in the center of the racket— never below the center— and send it *over* the net.

I want to underline this mistake of smashing into the net. It is tennis's main repeated error. Statisticians tell us that more than seven out of every ten missed smashes are hit into the net. Some people will take this lone statistic as sufficient warning. Others will no doubt prefer to have something more dramatic: they might like to learn that in the past eighty-odd years of lawn tennis history thousands and thousands of smashes have been sent down into the net,

71

almost all of them needlessly exchanging a winning position for a lost point.

BASIC ACTION FOR THE SMASH

Of the smaller proportion of smashes that go out, few indeed are aimed too high over the net. Almost every one of them has been hit somewhat below the **center** of the strings. Those that go into the back fence or raise a loud cheer by sometimes even clearing it on the full are hit from the bottom of the strings, down near the frame.

The basic cause of hitting in this danger area lies in taking your racket back too late. You should prepare early for your smash—using the mimimum of action helps here, too—and then time your forward hit so that it will not be too early and send the ball down into the net.

In the air or on the ground?

Opinions differ on whether you should smash from the ground or in the air. Some players say that keeping your back foot on the ground until you have hit the ball gives you that steady platform mentioned earlier and hence a safer feeling all round. The air adherents say that when you have to wait for a slow ball to drop, your timing is probably easier and certainly more positive if you rise to meet it instead of having the feeling that it is falling on top of you. They say that balance can be adjusted better when you are in the air than when you are anchored on the ground, and that since you are forced to take many smashes off the ground anyway, it is better to make this your normal method.

Personally, I recommend always going into the air, the deciding argument being that it gives you more positive timing. Although this is only a preference, I can take the definite view that going into the air is not unsafe technique. Nor is it flashy, smart, or showy in any way. Shy young players please note.

Perhaps you do not fancy the idea of *hitting the back of the ball* because it is at such a height that you feel you could easily hit it out. Well, I suppose you will agree that you cannot hit the top of it, or it will bounce down at your feet. Perhaps you do not really hit the back of it because in a smash your racket face tends to come over the ball. Just the same, when you bear in mind all those smashes that have gone into the net all over the world for so many years, you won't be doing badly to aim at the back. If the lob is a very deep one you will find that, if anything, you even have to aim a fraction below the back of the ball to get it over the net and send it deep enough.

How hard to hit a smash

How hard should you fire this big gun? As hard as you like, provided you never miss it. Unless you are right off balance, do not smash softly. It is no safer to be gentle with it; rather is it likely to be less safe because of "wobbliness," and it gives your opponent confidence that you cannot dispatch even his lobs. On the other hand, do not smash so hard that you are taking the slightest chance of missing.

Taking doubles as the best illustration, when one side is smashing and the other lobbing, the smashing side should win every such rally. More than in any other situation I can think of, they should never give the others a chance of getting off the hook—and to smash a good lob so hard that you can't be certain of playing it into court is to do exactly that. Smash every good lob you get at about three-quarter pace deep to somebody's backhand and move in again behind it. You won't get many good lobs in succession, so it's not as though you have to exercise a great deal of patience Eventually your opponents will toss out or short. When a short one comes I think it safer to smash it hard than to angle it or drop it short. If it's so short that you couldn't possibly hit it into the net and you are feeling fit and well, the treatment is to try and bounce it over the back fence. Flash? No. It takes concentration and accuracy, and that is just what you need on shots that are both easy and easily missed.

As a general policy, *do not let lobs bounce.* There might be exceptional circumstances such as a very high, almost vertical short lob, a strong wind, or night tennis, but, normally, allowing the bounce is tactically bad. It gives away the good position you already have and can send you so far back that you may need to make a winner in one hit. The sound policy is to take lobs on the fly.

A smash is nearly always made against an easy ball. When you get the feel of it, any time you like to concentrate on hitting the middle and sending the ball past the net you can go all afternoon without missing a solitary one. This is handy enough in singles; in doubles, where a lot more tossing goes on, it is money in the bank.

Emerson solidly blocks a forehand volley,
using the Continental grip.
(See text, page 99)

Turning sideways, Stan Smith punches a backhand volley.
(See text, page 99)

CHAPTER FIVE

Effective ground strokes

Foundation/Spin/Faults and remedies

For best results, modern ground strokes need to be founded on flat or slightly rolled shots, with more topspin for angle or dip, and slice for control only as required. They should also be based on taking the ball just after the top of the bounce, and earlier if necessary.

The reason—regardless of whether players are taught it early or come to learn it by defeat and experience—is that the net is the place to be if it can be gained after any stroke that is awkward for their opponents. The champion's serves are so good that he can go to the net on every one. At all costs he has to avoid services that are too weak to be followed in—otherwise he immediately loses the net position to the receiver who will follow in after his return of service. The champion cannot afford to let this happen.

The majority of the rest of us either come in behind a good serve or very soon after, or else we float about like watchful hawks waiting for the first short one to send back awkwardly and then follow it. About the only two groups of people who should not be at the net at every opportunity are the very young, who are too small to cover it and not strong enough in the wrist to volley properly, and the very old, for whom stretching and consequent weakening can make it a losing strategy.

It is true that in country towns you still often see players staying on the baseline when the net is theirs for the taking. Only where these players have very good ground strokes indeed, including control of angles and variation of pace, do they ever seriously trouble the city visitors to their local tournaments.

Against all this net-play, ground strokes based on under-spin shots will not do; nor is there any reason, these days, for a player to build his ground strokes on them. Modern tennis balls wear well and retain enough weight for flat or slightly rolled shots to be standard rather than ambitious.

The limitations of topspin

Heavy topspin is a great weapon against net players, but should not be made the basis of your ground shots. It is too tiring and as a general rule is not good for depth. Though it often makes a ball drop just in when otherwise it would have gone out, and this seems to equate with depth, a moment's thought should show you that the more spin you put on a ball the less certain you can be of exactly where it will land. Better still, of course, is to spend five minutes experimenting on the court, where I think you will find that when depth is required a flatter stroke is the right one to use.

The inadequacy of underspin

Underspin shots—particularly the small mild cut and the heavily spun chop, but also the longer lightly spun slice—are not good enough against a net-man. Cuts have little power, chops hang in the air too long, and slices travel at a steady height without much drop. These factors make all of them easy to volley unless they are perfectly controlled shots, and they are difficult to angle past a net-man without going over the sideline.

When your opponent is on the baseline, however, they can be useful strokes to have. They are steady, they probably take less effort to make against high and very low balls than any other stroke. Their natural swerve can be used to swing wide towards the sidelines, and as net-approach shots, where they are usually called chip shots, they can provide added

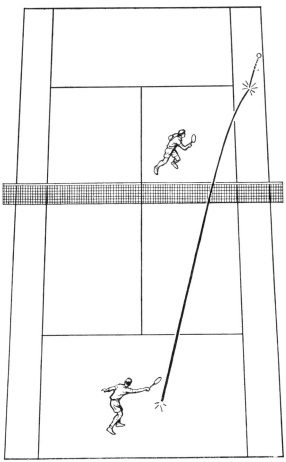

UNDERSPIN STROKE AGAINST A NET-PLAYER

If it passes the net-player it is likely to go over the sideline, especially when, as shown, the ball is hit a little on the inside and so tends to swerve outwards. Near-misses occur less from bad luck than from the odds being against these strokes.

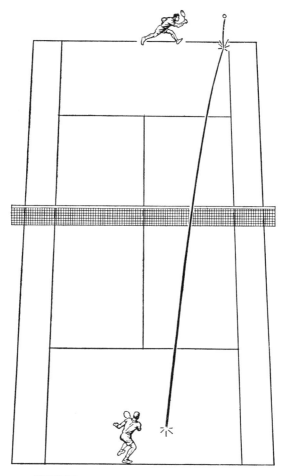

UNDERSPIN STROKE AGAINST A BASELINE PLAYER

Depth gained with little effort. The swerve obtained by
hitting inside the ball would put the shot within reach
of a player at the net, but against a player at the
baseline it makes the stroke more penetrating.

control and give you more time to take up the best net position.

Spin should not be neglected. If you cannot hit topspin and underspin strokes, your game will never be flexible. If, however, you aim to make either of them the foundation of your game you will find that underspin is a losing technique against net play and that excessive topspin, like Saturday's child, works hard for its living.

The flat drive

Is there such a thing as a completely flat drive? Hardly. When you are standing beside the court you very seldom see a ball go by with the brand on it facing you steadily for the whole of the ball's flight. From a flat drive it is always turning forward, even if slowly. The reason is that even when the ball is met with a square-on racket face the racket itself rises slightly in the follow-through, and thus some degree of forward spin is always imparted.

The important thing, however, is in the feel. You can feel yourself hitting a flat drive, pressing the ball as flat as it will go and sending it deep to the baseline, just as you can distinctly feel yourself putting some definite roll on it when, say, you want to send it shorter and cross-court.

Rising ball play

Is there such a thing as a true rising-ball player? Only in table-tennis. Even the greatest rising-ball artists in tennis still take more shots on the drop than on the rise.

Taking the ball on the rise as necessary gives you a tremendous advantage in time and position and, when you take these shots comfortably they look in a class by themselves.

Trying to take the ball on the rise all the time produces some opposite effects. There is no variation in the extra time you gain, so that your opponent becomes accustomed to it; you make needless errors; you get involved in many shots that are really somewhere between a half-volley and a normal rising-ball shot; finally, you grope as often as you stroke, so that instead of looking like the polished stylist of your imagination, you look more like a man who has no forehand at all and who is scrambling rather than driving.

Don't overdo it. Even racehorses aren't racing all the time.

If I had to choose one shot in cricket that had to be the basis of a batsman's game it would be the straight bat against a good-length ball. If the same narrow choice were forced on me in tennis I would say that the basic shot was the slightly rolled* forehand taken just after the top of the bounce. But do not restrict even your ground-stroke game to this alone. If all tennis players confined themselves to one basic shot there would be no more players like Arthur Ashe, and the game would die out in a season— deservedly.

So far we have been talking ideals. Now it is time to come down to what we are, to look at faults in stroke-production, and to consider suitable remedies.

There are many good club players who have a fine all-court game and appear to have all the strokes. They play a good positional game and are hard to beat. In reality, however, they have relatively poor forehands that do not match the rest of their games. It is to this type of player that the following forehand discussion is particularly addressed.

Good players with poor forehands always have a natural forehand stroke production that tends to send the ball too high. To keep the ball in court when they are under pressure, they play their forehands softer and softer. We will first discuss some direct causes of this inbuilt upward tendency and possible remedies—any one of which may suit your own case—then follow with a number of common forehand faults.

---

* Perhaps it will help some players if they regard this as forward spin, as distinct from the more up-and-over action of topspin. It is a more all-purpose shot than a flat drive could ever be.

Keeping the forehand low

Early backswing. Starting your backswing too late is one direct cause of a high-trajectory forehand. The racket goes round in a hurried loop and is often on the way up as it meets the ball.

It is sound practice to take your racket back the moment your brain registers which side the ball is coming to. Take, for example, playing a wide slow ball. Your racket should be behind you as you move across, waiting to swing forward. You should not move over carrying your racket in front of you and start your backswing after your arrival. The old advice to get your racket back early applies as much to advanced players as it does to beginners.

When you play on a court where the ball bounces higher than usual, make this early backswing a little higher too, but not so high that it will turn your drive into a slice.

Steady left hip. Turning your body to the front before contact also causes the ball to go higher than intended. It makes you bring your wrist through ahead of the racket, which in turn tends to open the racket face and send the ball up. An unfortunate aspect of this habit of turning before you hit the ball is that if you have no idea you are doing it, then the harder you try to play well the more you are likely to turn yourself round.

The remedy is to keep a rigid left hip, so get sideways-on to the ball and make the path of your racket travel from hip to hip. You might like to start by putting your left hand out towards the ball, as we discussed in the suggested action for smashing.

Weight co-ordination. Obviously if you lean back instead of forward as you hit the ball you will hit it up. This, like turning before hitting, amounts to your arm losing the assistance of your weight. Some readers may never have used their weight; others may have temporarily lost their natural knack of doing so and may not know what is wrong.

Here is a good way to get weight co-ordination, whether you have never had it or have temporarily lost it. Standing near the baseline, ask whomever you are practicing with to stand at the net and hit you a series of short ones. With very little backswing and only a flat racket, run forward into each of these and carry or send the ball straight back, following up to the net after each one. Just run the ball over the net.

Next, have your friend hit them a little deeper so that you have only, say, a couple of forward steps to make to reach the ball. Take a little longer backswing, and don't bother to follow up to the net. Then ask him to hit them deeper and deeper until finally you are playing from the back of the court, using a longer backswing, and not running forward to the ball *but* sending your weight naturally forward with every shot you hit.

Never worry about whether you start your forehand off the left or the right foot; but if you finish it with the weight still on the right foot you should worry.

Racket center. A further general cause of sending the ball too high is our old enemy, hitting the ball below the center of the racket—that is, down towards the throat. With overhead strokes I hope the discussion was easy enough to follow. With "sideways" strokes such as a forehand where the racket is horizontal (that is, reacket head level with wrist) I suggest you experiment for yourself, but here is the way I think you will find it.

Hit the middle of the racket, and besides securing power the ball tends to go at the height aimed. Hit a fraction higher than the center towards the top of the racket (away from the throat), and the power is naturally reduced a little, but not necessarily the control. True, the ball travels a little lower than you intended, but provided you get it over the net this is an extra safety margin which is quite noticeable and can be most useful when you are trying to hit yourself out of trouble from an awkward position.

If this seems to be getting a little involved don't pursue it. Just let me emphasize the real point at issue: that when you hit lower than the center the ball goes higher than you aimed. The only explanation I can offer for this is that the racket head has not had time to get round to the correct position for sending the ball where you aimed, which was forward and low.

Forward follow-through. Although your racket is correctly horizontal at impact, the ball can unintentionally be lifted upward if your natural swing is somewhat too circular and you hit the ball a fraction too late in the rising part of your forward swing.

The obvious remedy here is to take a flatter swing, so by all means try this. If it feels comfortable your worries should be over. You may, however, be so grooved into your natural circular swing that the new one will feel artificial and unreliable—and weak, as though you were pushing at the ball. If so, you can retain your natural swing and so be able to move quickly and instinctively as ever, modifying it only as your racket meets the ball by sending the racket head definitely out ahead of you instead of letting it rise too sharply. This might also influence you not to let your own head come up too soon either.

Aiming at the net. Lastly, perhaps you are a player who has a forehand that is good when played from low or dropping balls but poor on high balls. You drive confidently only from below net height and cannot believe it when you are told that a waist-high ball must be the easiest because it only needs to be hit straight past the net.

This simply means that your natural stroke is played with a lifting follow-through. You have found in the past that when playing balls net-high or higher you lifted them too high over the net and over the baseline, and as a result you have changed to a different action to play high balls. This action is probably more downward, and perhaps a trace of unwanted slice creeps into it now and then; at all events it has never become as natural to you as the lifting action you use so well on low balls.

If these circumstances apply to you, and you feel it is too late in your tennis life for fundamental change, you should try playing your natural lifting follow-through on balls of all heights. For balls net-high or above you will have to set yourself as though you were driving into the net, and then lift the ball to clear it.

Strange cases invite strange remedies. Give yourself a chance, however. Start with low balls and build up to high balls and you may have found the answer.

Common faults

When it comes to handling detailed faults, the best way might be to describe a sound backhand and then contrast it with the forehand. This may simplify self-criticism.

On the backhand, then, our imaginary player has a feeling of control in his fingers, no matter what his grip is technically called. He takes his racket back early. Either his footwork or his hip-turning is good—at all events he gets the ball coming up nicely beside him, giving him more time to absorb its speed than if he stood square-on and hurriedly hit at it somewhere in front of him. With a straight arm, keeping his wrist low, he brings the racket head round his wrist outside and over the ball. This is as though he had the ball trapped between his racket and himself where it cannot get away until he sends it on its path, easing out his slightly bent knees for weight and power. He seems to be as smooth as a panther. What a pity we have to look at his forehand side as well.

Over on the right side our player clubs the racket handle hard down into the depths of his fist. Not only is he taut as he swings forward but he was just as taut, as well as being late, in his preceding backswing. He does not get his head down over the ball as he does on the backhand, so that he does not see the ball after it is about three feet from his strings. His knees are straight when he drives, even though he unknowingly uses them very well for a lob, which is his best shot on the forehand side.

Accustomed to turning sideways with the ball when he plays a backhand, he does not make much of a turn at all on the forehand. To make up for this lack of turn and still meet the ball squarely, he has to push his wrist forward;

this tends to make him hit the ball below the center of the racket and up it goes. He finds himself using more and more topspin to bring down balls that he never intended to go high. His arm was bent as he hit the ball, his right shoulder hunched, his stroke cramped. . . .

If our imaginary player looked like a panther on one side I have made him appear a positive cripple on the other. No one would be quite like that, of course, but good players with inadequate forehands always have some of the faults described.

I am not proposing that you should burden yourself with being conscious of every fault I have covered. All you are looking for is the one thing that particularly applies to you and is preventing your forehand from being effective.

Let me remind you that this has been written to help players who have a poor forehand. Please do not confuse this with a forehand that is poorly produced in some way or other. If you have a forehand that contains any of the faults I have been describing and yet is most effective you may try improving it further, but you must not spoil it. Not under any circumstances.

The player who has tried everything

There is one man among the group of good all-round players with poor forehands whom I would very much like to help. He is the player who has already tried every known remedy. Each week he picks up a new idea. He tries it, and it works, but then something else goes wrong. By this time he is thoroughly confused and is coming to the conclusion that the forehand is the one stroke he will never master.

He won't master it either, if he keeps adding to it and subtracting from it chip by chip. It is probably years since he made one natural movement in this shot. By now it is completely synthetic and artificial. He should take heart, however, because if he is capable of making all the other strokes in tennis he must be capable of making this one.

He has to shuffle the cards and make a new deal. He

should choose a period where there are no matches coming up; get a new racket or restring; go on to the court with a friend and hit every ball, forehand and all, as hard as he can. Hitting at his very hardest must force him to be natural. By playing this way several times and not bothering scoring, his correct or instinctive forehand should be born. Quietening it down a little for respectable control, he should then forget the previous methods he tried were ever part of his game.

This is radical—recommended for those who feel they have succeeded in building up nothing they cannot afford to lose.

Forehand wrist action

Many players are uncertain about the forehand wrist action they should adopt. On the backhand the wrist unrolls itself naturally, but with their forehands some players never know from one week to another if they are using too much or too little. Among the champions, some are described as having a firm wrist, others as having a beautifully free wrist action. At the same time the equivalent forehand drives of lesser lights are respectively described as being as stiff as a poker, or as flicking or having a wrist-waggle. The question is, where do the differences lie, and, while we are at it, how much wrist should be used anyway?

Please get out your racket. Stand sideways to an imaginary net and take the racket back until it is straight in line with your shoulders. Hold your wrist and elbow straight and bring your arm slowly round as straight as an iron bar. That is what is meant by as stiff as a poker. Take your arm back exactly as before and this time relax your elbow a little as you bring your arm forward. The difference is more in the elbow than in the wrist, and that is how a drive with a firm wrist is made—in theory.

Now take your racket back quickly, pause, and have a look at it. You will see that the weight of the racket head has taken the head a little farther back than dead in line with your arm and two shoulders; in other words, without

U.S. L.T.A. photograph

Emerson volleys well in front—for rigidity and a
good view of the ball.
(See text, page 100)

". . . Sauce for the gander." Note the similarity of Margaret Court's
high volley to Hoad's contact on page 172.
(See text, page 100)

your trying for it or even being aware of it, a little wrist action was automatically built into the backswing. Swing forward with your arm straight yet not rigid. That is how the firm-wrist drive is made in practice. It is perfectly correct, smooth, and very sound; and it is the method a coach would normally teach.

Now let's try to contrast good and bad "wristy" swings. Stand sideways to the net and take your racket back in line with your shoulders once more. This time bend your wrist back as far as it will comfortably go. Swing slowly forward, elbow straight yet not rigid, reducing the wrist angle (that is, the amount by which the racket head trails behind) until it is nearly all gone at the point of impact with an imaginary ball. Combined with a smooth follow-through, this is a correct free-wristed drive.

Flicking means leaving all the wrist-angle on until just before contact and then . . . well, flicking your racket head quickly at the ball.

One more self-demonstration with your racket, this time of wrist-waggle, and we have finished. Take the racket back straight in line with your shoulders, keeping your wrist straight. Bring it slowly forward again, but increase the wrist-angle until it is at its maximum at the point of impact. To hit the ball straight you can see that you have to turn your body round towards the net before you contact the ball, weakening your power. Probably the old side-effects of the elbow sliding in towards ribs and the right shoulder hunching will also be there. Do all this quickly and let your racket head waver up and down a bit as well and you will have manufactured for yourself as good an example of a wrist-waggling drive as could be found anywhere.

Of the correct solid-wrist and free-wrist drives, which is preferable? The solid-wrist must be sounder, and its users would have few off-days. Played by a champion on a good surface, it would look as though it could seldom be missed. The free-wristed drive requires better timing, but it has its own advantages; it permits last-second change of direction, better concealed change of pace, and easier adjustment to a bad bounce.

I hope both styles continue to be used. It takes two to make a tennis match, and there is nothing better to see than a good match between two players alike in power, smoothness, and sportsmanship but whose styles contrast in straight or "wristy" strokes. If really pressed to state a preference—and that is all it can be—I would say that, much as I admire straight shots that go across a lawn court like billiard balls along a green table, even more do I like to see them guided there from a free wrist. But make your own choice for your own game. As with everything in tennis, be your own man or you will be lost against fast play.

This also really answers the query on how much wrist you should use. Just please yourself. How much wrist you *can* use depends, just as pace does, on how much you can control. The more wrist you use, the more speed and flexibility you can get for the same effort, up to a certain point. Beyond that point too much effort begins to be needed to control the wrist itself.

I am not saying that you really ought to use as much wrist as you can control. True, you can get that extra speed, but, as indicated earlier, you make your timing more difficult. To make my meaning clearer, let us suppose that someone asks what is the ideal swing and can it ever be achieved?

The ideal would be a swing so smooth that the racket head traveled at the same speed throughout the length of the stroke. This is not possible, because in practice the racket head has to travel at its fastest just before meeting the ball. In the almost perfect stroke, therefore, this part of the swing is as slightly as possible faster than the rest of the swing, which in turn can only be when the racket head trails as little behind the wrist as possible; and this equates with the firm-wristed drive.

Strengthening the backhand

Much of the preceding forehand discussion can be applied equally to the backhand.

Strong backhands are always made with a straight arm at the point of impact and usually with the racket face coming slightly outside and over the ball.

Backhands made with a bent elbow, cramped too close to the body, are invariably weak. Those made by hitting inside and under the ball are nearly always so.

Probably the root cause of a weak backhand lies in an *inadequate grip,* a grip not sufficiently behind the handle to give enough support. As I have said, most players with such a grip either take the ball somewhere beside their bodies and produce a small cut stroke, or take it in the normal place, a little in front of the right hip, but because of their grip the wrist is in front of the handle and the arm is bowed. In either case very little power can be obtained.

If you have this inadequate grip and you are going to stick to it, the only way to improve matters and have a straight arm and low wrist with the racket head coming round and over the ball is to turn well sideways and take the ball farther behind you than you may ever have thought possible. This will place a fair amount of strain on your wrist, but it will permit you to make a rolled backhand and will almost certainly improve your backhand side to some degree.

And here you leave it, content that you have strengthened your shot without having altered what has been your natural grip. Perhaps you leave it. It is more likely you will feel that changing your grip just a little more will be well worth doing. In passing, should you not know it already, you change grip mainly by the use of your left-hand fingers on the throat of the racket. In the time it takes to get the racket back the grip can be easily changed.

A common misconception with the backhand is that it needs a long backswing. In making this long swing many players run short of time and have to hurry the forward swing. Haste always results in inconsistency, and so (here we have our common tennis fallacies again) these players get the despondent idea that they were born to have an erratic backhand.

Provided you have changed grip sufficiently, the wrist will be definitely stronger on the backhand than on the forehand, so for the same speed you do not need as long a backswing on your backhand side. This in turn gives you that extra time and adds to your backhand confidence.

The era of two-handed backhand players demonstrated this most clearly. Some of us single-handers may have thought it was the extra strength from using two hands that permitted the short backswing. But most of us thought that nothing the two-handers did applied to us, and so we did not examine this shot. The champions, as always ever hungry to learn, did examine it, and we have not seen long-backswing backhand play from them for years. Many people seeing the champions' short backhand backswing may think it's entirely due to their receiving a lot of fast balls. I think there's more to it than that. I fancy that the two-handers showed them the way.

Forehand and backhand balance

It is a great advantage if your forehand and backhand are fairly well balanced, particularly against those weakness-probing, net-hunting players who are commoner these days than they ever were before. The forehand should be the stronger side. If it is not, you should search for the reason and rectify it, because a player capable of a good backhand should normally be capable of an even better forehand. However, in achieving this balance between strokes by building up the weaker one, never neglect the stronger. The saying that a chain is only as strong as its weakest link does not apply to tennis. Keep your strong links. Neglect a good stroke long enough and you will lose it. This sounds most obvious advice, but even champions, whom I have been

A really low volley. Dennis Ralston bends his knees
and keeps his wrist low rather than drop his racket head.
The easiest place to hit a low volley is into the net;
Ralston forces this one over.

(See text, page 100)

Low volley. Arthur Ashe bends his knees and has his racket
almost horizontal. This is safe technique 'for timing
and a better sight of the ball.
(See text, page 103)

holding up as paragons of tennis virtue until now, have made this mistake.

In balancing your strokes, try to keep them as much as possible as a pair. Players who produce forehands and backhands in similar fashion have fewer off-days on either or both wings. However, even if you roll one and slice the other, at least try to be comfortable in taking both at the same height. Otherwise there'll be no spot where you'll really like to stand to receive service, particularly in doubles, but also against a man who follows a fast serve to the net in singles.

In a way the forehand and backhand are a little like male and female. Male strength and female support is a fairly acceptable idea. Further, although the male is generally accepted as being the stronger and more able to take hard knocks, it is also the male who is more likely to become wayward and who is definitely harder to bring back to the fold, while the female, once developed and settled, goes fairly peacefully along.

Build up a strong forehand or hold fast to the good one you have. Even if your opponents are going to do everything possible to shut your forehand out of the game, going into a match without one makes you feel like a cowboy without his gun.

Aids to ground-stroke steadiness

If at any stage you do not feel confident of your ground strokes, try one of the following aids to steadiness:
- Watch the ball till you stop it.
- Get your racket back early enough to have a pause.
- Have your elbow straight as you hit the ball.
- Hold the ball on the strings.

Recalling ball-watching to mind always reduces the apparent speed of your opponent's game. Having time for a fractional pause before hitting gives you a feeling of being master of your fate. Having a straight arm at impact provides a wonderful measuring-stick at a time when everything seems astray. Holding the ball on the strings is a great confidence-builder when the ball seems to be an elusive enemy instead of a close friend.

CHAPTER SIX

Volleys, drop shots, lobs

Use/Technique/Touch

Volleys

Volleys are crisp strokes. To match that fact, here are some short, sharp, generally accepted facts about them:

Most balls are more easily and effectively hit on the fly than on the bounce. Volleying mainly consists of blocking fast ones and punching slow ones. The Continental is possibly the best grip to use. Always try to volley in front of your body, and from higher than the net. When forced to volley low, get down to the ball and use a horizontal racket.

In case these remarks have given you mental indigestion, we'll take them more slowly.

Except for a viciously topspun stroke, just about everything within reach is easier to take on the full than on the bounce. The reason players are not at the net all the time is that some returns could be out of reach, not that they would be too fast. However good your ground strokes, you have the ability to volley better again.

At the net there are points for the taking; not to volley means not to win your share.

Blocking and punching are the orthodox and easy volleying techniques, but if you have a vigorous drive volley for high balls you should keep it. It may often bring the hearts of your well-wishers into their mouths with apprehension, but it will have a similar effect on your opponents.

Continental-grip players nearly always volley well, mainly because they have to make little or no change of grip from forehand to backhand and low balls present little difficulty.

Many Eastern players use the Continental grip for their volleys. If you volley well with the Eastern grip, stay that way. If you feel you are rather clumsy, you can modify your volleying grips so that there is less change from forehand to backhand, but you must be prepared to find that you have somewhat less power.

Volleying above and below the net

Volleying the ball farther in front of you than where you would position yourself for a drive gives a greater rigidity and a far better view of the ball. This clear sight of the target is probably the more important reason of the two.

When you volley from above the net, the easiest place to hit the ball is into the court. You must believe this, for it enhances your confidence and encourages you to go forward and make high volleys whenever possible. Most of the volleys you miss go near the top of the net or near the lines; it is easier to hit the ball into the large court than to go close to the net-band or sidelines. With volleys that are high and slow, however, make sure you are well side-on (slide your front foot well forward) or the easiest thing of all is to hook or slice them across court and a long way out near the side fence.

On the other hand, when you volley from below net level the natural odds are no longer with you because the easiest place to hit a low volley is straight into the net. I'm not saying that you or anyone else hit most low volleys into the net instead of into the court, only that into the net is the easiest place to hit them; and if you care to observe it you will certainly find most missed low volleys go into the net. You have to cradle them over at the right height and to the right depth as well. This calls for definite method and touch.

We dealt with this matter of *touch* in the chapter on ball control, saying that in low-volleying fast balls close to the net you not only have to get them over, you also have

Whether they know it or not, many players are stronger—
and most are swifter—when volleying on the backhand side.
Pancho Gonzales is late with his right foot,
but his weight is going forward.
(See text, page 103)

Tony Roche is a lefthander who does turn sideways for his backhand volley. It has been rated the world's best.
(See text, page 104)

to absorb some of their speed or they will fly well over the baseline.

Coming to method, you should play as many low volleys as possible with your racket in a horizontal position—that is, with the racket head level with the wrist, no matter how low they are. With a *horizontal racket,* you need only reasonable timing to direct the ball to the desired height low over the net, whereas with a perpendicular racket the timing would need to be exact. It is not difficult to see that if you swung the racket in underarm (perpendicular) fashion at the ball there would be very little difference in timing between a volley that went along the ground and one that went much too high over the net. So when players get right down to their low volleys they are being practical rather than stylish.

Another important reason why you must get down to low volleys is that you then see them better. It is a matter of eye-level, and apparently it is an optical fact that the nearer the ball is to your eye-level the better you can see it. You can't very well get your eye right down to the level of a low volley, but by getting well down and keeping the racket head horizontal you can get the level as close as practically possible. However, in getting down you cannot bring your eye closer to the ball level by bending your back, because if you did this you would overbalance; the technique is to keep your back straight and bend your knees, sometimes to their fullest extent. Don't bend your back. Squat.

There is another type of volley with which special care needs to be taken if it is to go over the net. This is the *volley that is nearly out of reach.* When you stretch out and just manage to reach the ball you get very little power behind it. Make sure you give it more lift than usual.

Many competent volleyers do not realize how good their *backhand volley* is. Feeling that they have extra power and reach on the forehand, they do not see that the backhand volley is actually the sounder of the two in several conditions, such as when volleying close to the middle of the body and when volleying low near the feet. Further, if you happen to be close to the net when your opponent is smashing, the backhand volley is probably the fastest reflex action you have; when standing with the throat of your racket in your left hand your racket is already in position for a waist-high backhand volley.

Awareness of all this improves confidence in your backhand volley, and as a result you play it better.

Volley for angles if you are going to win with that one shot; otherwise you usually give your opponent a good chance of passing you. Use drop-volleys and toss-volleys sparingly, or in the final reckoning they will be found to have cost more than they paid. Volleying deep should be your main aim.

In general, I think left-handers, being used to having plenty of time with their forehand drives, tend to take too long a backswing with their forehand volleys. They would do better with their backhand volleys if they turned side-on to the net more. I give this as an opinion from playing against them.

Half-volleys are part of your armory

Do not be frightened of executing a half-volley shot deliberately every now and then, and never be at all worried when you are forced into one. *Played close to the ground* the half-volley is quite a natural shot, and once you are satisfied about that most of the difficulty disappears.

We used to be told to half-volley from necessity only and always to use our feet to go either forward or back to avoid the shot whenever possible. This may be all very well in some ways, but it gets you into a frame of mind where you almost feel your opponent has out-generalled you whenever you have to play a half-volley. This is a defeatist attitude and amounts to placing a heavy and unfair load on one of your own strokes.

Deliberate half-volleying can well be used in at least two situations that come to mind. When you're approaching the net, a half-volley is easier than a volley that is so low that it can't be hit in the center of the strings. Rather than stretch forward to the last inch, it is often more comfortable to pause fractionally and half-volley the ball, thereby keeping in better balance.

There is also the deep half-volley. If, as you have already seen, you should take all lobs on the full to avoid retreating for a perhaps stronger shot but one which loses your position, then why shouldn't this argument apply to deep half-volleys? When you happen to be, say, just inside the baseline and a deep return comes along, it is better to half-volley it than to run round behind it and attempt to drive from a position well behind the baseline. You couldn't very well tell a beginner that, but sooner or later we all have to grow up in tennis, just as our opponents do.

Play your half-volleys as close to the ground as possible and go into them with confidence. Do not hesitate or play them reluctantly or you are likely to get involved in the horrible shot that is somewhere between a half-volley and a rising ball. So far as I know, this shot is nameless—at any rate in print.

The safest method—when you have the time—is to use a horizontal racket head level with your wrist, knees well bent, backswing short, a definite follow-through, and long contact for control. Note particularly—and, of course, try them out on the court—the long contact and follow-through, for many players think of half-volleys only as quickly stabbed shots.

When half-volleys are forced on you, near the net and straight at your feet, you may have no choice but to play them with a vertical racket. In these circumstances be as quick as you can, and good luck to you. Even with these, though, I maintain they will be handled far better by a man who occasionally half-volleys deliberately than by one who plays this stroke from strict necessity only.

Whatever you do, don't over indulge in deliberate half-volleys. Don't play more and more from choice the very stroke that a veteran plays more and more each year from necessity. After all, one of the tests of a good return of service against a man coming in to the net is that it gives him a volley which is low; if it makes him half-volley it is even better. Further, the direction of a half-volley is often easier for your opponent to anticipate than that of either a low volley or a ground stroke. For example, a backhand half-volley is nearly always played cross-court.

Another important reason is that half-volley specialists tend to become lackadaisical and even sloppy. Without being forced to do so they sometimes half-volley from the baseline with a vertical racket. This is a relaxed stroke and may do no harm when your opponent is at the back of the court, but it seldom lends itself to the accuracy needed for a passing shot.

I can sense some modest man pondering this business of half-volleying deliberately, even if it is only done sometimes. Can it be sound? Doesn't it seem a bit up-stage? Couldn't it be regarded as—that terrible word flung at enterprising juniors—flash? Modesty is a fine thing, but don't let people turn you into a cart-horse. Go out and see the tennis world for yourself.

Drop shots

On a hard court, on a hot summer's day, and hitting downwind, forget them. On grass or all-weather courts, on a damp winter's day, and playing against the wind, you should use them at every opportunity. Adjust the frequency of use to the conditions varying between these two extremes.

This is a general guide only. Naturally, the best use of drop shots, or avoidance of them, is not covered by conditions alone. Other factors are involved: how good or bad you are at making them; how slow or how quick your opponent's anticipation is; the type of game he likes to play best (such as standing well back and sending over long pounding drives); and whether it is in your interests to keep the rallies going or to break them up at all costs.

Drop shots are definitely a part of the grass-court game, in which they can often be played with no great risk. This benefits the game of tennis as a whole and is partly responsible for the early-ball type of play that grass-court players develop. Where a drop shot is always likely, players have to be within striking distance. Under normal hard-court conditions a drop shot has to be much more finely done if it is to amount to much more than a very short ball, and so it is attempted far less frequently. This in turn is partly why the typical hardcourt player takes the ball later than the grass-court man, even though the former plays on a surface where a more regular bounce prevails.

Another reason for the rising-ball and dropping-ball styles of grass and hard-court players relate to the weight of the balls. As play continues the weight of the balls on a grass court tends to increase from picking up moisture from the grass, whereas on a hard court it decreases from wear. There is nothing better for confidence in rising-ball play than good solid balls with some weight in them.

I am sorry to have mentioned court surfaces, because it immediately involves me in associated explanation. By hard courts I mean the hard-packed natural yellow loam courts, and antbed courts too, of which there are hundreds in Australia and which in summertime are not unlike America's concrete courts; I do not mean the so-called hard courts of Europe, which are softer and slower than grass.

By grass courts I mean the average club-competition courts which are softer and often slower than hard courts; I do not mean the top championship courts, rolled to the maximum and closely shaved, that are found at Wimbledon, Forest Hills, White City, Kooyong, and elsewhere. Though these are certainly no harder than our hard courts, the ball travels faster on them because it comes off grass-roots which have less friction than the sandy content of hard-court surfaces. These championship grass courts are said to provide the second-fastest surface there is, the polished wood of indoor courts allegedly being the fastest. Unless the court is damp the balls have little chance of gaining much weight; they are changed after every nine games, not so much because their weight may have altered greatly in that short time, but mainly to have them at a constant compression.

Drop shot variation: Drop shots are, of course, touch shots. To play them, as with drop volleys or stop volleys—the broad difference between these two is that the drop volley is made from a slow ball and the stop volley by taking the pace right off a fast one—you need the "feel" of your fingers. Underspin gives best control and least bounce.

Once again, these should not be overdone. When your opponent anticipates one, it becomes no more than a short ball from which it is he who makes the winner. Then, in trying to get them finer and finer, what you finally find is the net. Often this means that you do more than lose the point—you lose it from a very weak shot, and that often lowers your confidence for the next point.

When your opponent plays a drop shot from fairly far back and you can reach it comfortably, a drop shot in return is often your easiest winner. When you cannot reach it comfortably and in contrast come in with the momentum of a railway train, then unless you have a certain winner across to either line it is best to play it deep and straight at your opponent—but not so deep that he can make a volley of it. Apply your brakes and try to cover a probable toss. The worst has happened if your opponent gets it over your head for a winner, especially if it is doubtful enough to make you chase it unsuccessfully. Such a combination of drop shot and toss always makes the master tactician feel very good and the victim very bad and somewhat ragged as well.

Negative and attacking lobbing

The lob is like religion. It has few vocal supporters, but few care to attack it in print; it is practiced comparatively little, yet people turn to it in moments of need. Too much of it is not generally considered manly (rightly or wrongly), yet the game—tennis or life—would be the poorer without it.

No one feeling a glow of self-satisfaction after a hard-fought and well-deserved victory remembers his lobs very much. In social or practice doubles people will usually try any more aggressive stroke, however ambitious, rather than

Rod Laver is nicely set for a backhand lob.
It's a pity the ball is not on the other side,
where he has a wicked lefthander's topspin lob.
(See text, page 112)

Rosie Casals' backhand smash confirms that you need not be tall,
nor even masculine.
(See text, pages 70, 113)

resort to a mere lob; this is such standard practice that players are liable to get into the habit of adopting a wrong net position because they do not have to bother much about guarding against a lob.

What a difference in a match! Hard-pressed, a man sends up a lob almost automatically.

Unless a lob has some element of attack in it, or is at least awkward enough to be difficult, the player who makes it is only hoping for the best. If his opponent shows that he can smash competently, the player doing the hoping has actually very little to hope for. To continue *defensive lobbing* is rather like hoisting the white flag. When continually pressed by a volleyer it is often far better to attempt more rising-ball topspin strokes. They can fare no worse than the lobs, and, even if all of them do not go in, your opponent has to guard against these angles and gets drawn closer to the net; it is then that you have a chance to play a toss with more initiative behind it.

Tennis would be much the poorer if lobs were not part of it. In doubles, particularly, the net could be crowded so closely as to become a virtually impregnable position. The game would become very dull and would never contain, for instance, those interesting passages where a player with fine ground-stroke control forces his opponent to half-volley and then tosses almost out of his reach, forcing a defensive smash which, followed in, results in his being met with yet another half-volley to play, and so on. There would be no more toss volleys, to be suddenly interjected during a rapid-fire net exchange. The lob plays its part as a foil, too; without lobs, no full-blooded smashes could be played.

Nearly all of us have two weaknesses in our lobbing or tossing, either in our use of the shot or in our production of it.

The lob, in itself, is a careful sort of stroke, and this tends to make us play it in a careful frame of mind so that we are frightened of hitting it out. Perhaps we instinctively recoil from the thought of not being able to hit an easy donkey-drop stroke into court. Whatever the reasons behind it, the result is that as a rule the average player tosses too short. Sometimes he gets away with it, though he never should, but when he does not it has that well-known effect of making him feel that he has lost more than the one point by adding to his opponent's confidence and detracting from his own.

Similarly, in our stroke production of the lob the attitude of care and safety-first manifests itself. For added control we play most of our lobs with underspin. This tends to keep our lobs from going out, but because it makes them hang in the air it also gives our opponents more time to cover them, whether on the full or in recovery after the bounce. Worse still, since we tend to toss too short anyway, the use of underspin makes our lobs even shorter. It sounds like a chapter of accidents.

We would be far better off if we learnt to play our *lobs with roll*. Our lob would then become a more manly stroke and would probably be worthy of some practice. It would certainly be a great deal more dangerous to an opponent.

Some players do have a heavy topspin lob as part of their stroke equipment, and this shot is a definite threat to any opponent. It is not easy to do and is mostly to be found amongst very free-wristed left-handers who, to balance a less effective backhand, have become experts on just about any stroke at all on the forehand side.

Without a rolled lob there are still several ways in which the ordinary toss can be used to attack. Whenever a man crowds in that little bit extra at the net to block off every possible angle, it is always just too far in, particularly if he loses his balance as well. Here a lob can often be an outright winner. In doubles, if the net man stands too close, the lob over his head, especially from the right court, should be the first stroke played, and it should be played repeatedly until such time as you feel he is going to cover it. Any reasonable lob which ends on your opponent's backhand side frequently acts as a source of attack. Few players have a backhand smash; instead, most play a more or less defensive high backhand volley which can pass the initiative to you.

Though no great admirer of the gentle art of tossing, I have to admit that the lob is a great old standby and workhorse. Worrying over our probable form for a coming match, it never enters our heads, yet in the heat of battle we always expect to be able to call on it at a second's notice.

CHAPTER SEVEN

Footwork, scrambling, stroking

Getting to the ball/How your strokes look

Footwork

However impeccable your stroke-making, you must get to the ball. Many players regard footwork as solely connected with the arrangement of their feet just before hitting the ball. This tends to make them relatively slow movers and can be most heartening to their opponents.

Footwork is not an end in itself. It is a means of making every ball you receive as easy to play as possible.

Your general aim should be to hurry neither your footwork nor your strokes, but you can do this only when you are clearly the stronger player. When you have to hurry, always hurry your footwork before your strokes. Sometimes you may be forced to hurry your strokes as well, but never do so from choice.

Some players, either in striving for calmness or in trying to give an opponent the impression that they have plenty in reserve, deliberately affect a lackadaisical type of footwork. This is a mistake. You get a better result if you move your feet quickly and arrive early, with your racket already back, as described previously, and then make a completely unhurried stroke. This keeps your strokes in good form, too Conversely, if you loaf with your footwork you can quite suddenly lose confidence in your strokes. Lazy footwork is normally the first sign of over confidence.

Fast footwork makes your opponent's game seem slower.

In placing your feet, the object is to be sideways to the net. The ideal is where a projected line drawn from the toe of the back foot to the toe of the front foot would be parallel to the intended line of flight of the ball, and that is how almost all players arrange their service stance.

Foot placement for ground strokes

With ground strokes things vary a little. When playing a short ball you merely step forward into it. With wider balls there are two alternative methods of placing your feet. You can choose either to hit across your front leg or hit along it.

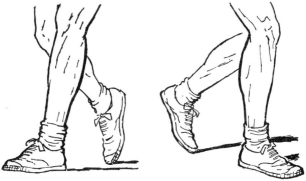

Forehand   Backhand

POSITION OF FEET WHEN HITTING ACROSS THE FRONT LEG

The older school maintained that a player should always advance his front foot to the ball—left for forehand and right for backhand. This, as you can see, means that the player hits wide balls across his front leg. I do not propose to say anything against this method. How can I, when its strongest supporter was none other than the famous American player, Bill Tilden, who was probably the greatest exponent of powerful forehand and backhand driving of all time? Pictures of this tall, masterful champion show him **practicing** what he preached. With his long arm back ready to slam his shot, his long front leg is always across to the ball. Further, leaving Tilden and the old school aside and looking at players we know, we find that shots mounted on a firmly based front foot are seldom weak.

Modern opinion grants that the foregoing method produces strong shots, but condemns it as not being flexible enough. Reach is restricted if you try to play a wide forehand ball from your left foot. Direction is less accurate if the two feet are not in line with the intended path of the ball. Finally, the leg crossed over in front of you slows your movement for the next shot, particularly if you intend to follow in to the net.

POSITIONING FOR A FOREHAND HIT ALONG THE FRONT LEG

The modern idea of forehand footwork is to step round the ball with the right foot and step forward with the left, thus hitting along the front leg instead of across it. Similarly, with the backhand, you step round the ball with the left foot and forward with the right, sending your weight along the right leg.

If you follow either the old method or the modern one you will have good footwork (or, to be more precise, good foot placement). Both methods bring your weight into your shots and give you good balance.

You have fair footwork if your stance is somewhat more open and you compensate by turning your hips more so that you are properly sideways to the net as you hit the ball. But you will have to use more effort to get the same power as a player with good footwork, and your balance at the end of the shot will not be as good.

You have poor footwork if your stance is so open that the following disadvantages are the result: first, that you can send the ball straight only by pushing your wrist forward; second, that your weight tends to stay on your right foot; third, that if you do succeed in getting your weight going forward you end by losing your balance because there is no front foot to maintain it.

Coming back to the two sound methods of foot placement, I think you will have realized that, in general, hitting across the front leg suits the long-swinging ground-stroke players, while hitting along the front leg seems to fit in with the rising-ball game.

Notwithstanding all this, if you look at present-day players you will see that they seem to use something from each method. Most play the forehand along the front leg and the backhand across the front leg. This must be the most natural way, showing that both the old and the modern schools may have been a shade too theoretical when each laid down a single rule for the best footwork on both forehand and backhand.

The neglected art of scrambling

Some people have a mistaken idea that a good player should never scramble, or that if he does, then the worse the footwork form the better the result.

On the first point, Tilden, high priest of orthodox stroke-play in the Eastern American style, once went so far as to say that the test of a true champion was his ability to scramble. On the second, you can play anything you like from the right foot because in the case of scrambling it is not unorthodox form. From your right foot you can reach those extra few inches in any direction—forehand or backhand, behind you or in front. When going for a wide, low forehand ball, where you will have very little power and will have to slice to even get round it, make your last stride with the right leg intentionally; the wide-open stance will always tend to lift the ball for you. When lobbing in recovering smashes with very little time available to you, play off either foot; but always try to get one or other of them on the ground before you hit the ball.

In organizing your footwork for volleying, the more sideways-on a position that rapid footwork can give you, the less backswing you will need for the same power; and less backswing means greater accuracy and safety. If there is no time to move your feet, thrust your weight forward just before impact. With high volleys there is nearly always ample time to turn sideways, and you already know that it is courting disaster not to do so.

Left-handers have their own characteristics in footwork, one being that many of them seem to abhor straight lines. In soccer these people have a left-footer's hook and in bowling a cricket ball they often make their approach at an angle and once again propel the ball rather round the corner. In tennis they tend to do the opposite and stand more square-on to the net than a right-hander normally does. They play many forehands by advancing the left foot to the ball and can hit down-the-line from a stance that would normally indicate a cross-court shot. They manage to keep their cross-court forehands in by very good control of topspin, and we could note in passing how these off-line left-handers have a marked preference for topspin rather than straight strokes.

That is the way of many left-handers, and it would be a rash man indeed who criticized a good left-hander's fore-

No champion can be a fair-weather player.
Billie Jean King copes with a bad bounce.
(See text, page 130)

Scrambling is part of the game. Champion John Newcombe is not too proud to do his share. (See text, page 118)

hand. But—and it is a solid *but*—the laws of footwork demand to be recognized, and over on the backhand side nearly all square-on left-handers pay a heavy price for neglecting them.

If you are a left-hander you should practice placing your left foot well across for the backhand. Point your left shoulder to the net; in fact, while learning to turn adequately you can practically turn your back on it. I do not know of any way of having a strong backhand with square-on footwork.

Lastly, there are many players whose foot-placement is good on one side and poor on the other. In many cases they are slower (unnecessarily) in getting to the ball on their poorer side. This gets us back to where we came in. Right-handed, left-handed, double-handed, ambidextrous, or unevenly balanced with foot placement—first catch your hare. Always get to the ball quickly, then carry on from there.

The arm without a racket

We don't have to give the left arm too much sympathy. After all, it never does enough work to have a sore wrist, tennis-elbow, or a stiff shoulder. On the other hand, it is working all the time, and mostly working unnoticed. Though some players are conscious of it and have developed their styles to make the most use of it without further thought, many are hardly aware that they use it for much more than throwing up the ball to serve.

I have mentioned its use earlier in a few particular instances, and, taken all round, it is certainly a great steadier and balancer. Balance leads to smoothness. Some people may be inclined to dismiss smoothness as something of possible appeal only to onlookers, whereas all they themselves are interested in is having a good strong game with plenty of power, whether it is smooth or not. I hope that in the time it has taken you to read as far as this you will have realized how closely smoothness and power are connected. For the same effort, the smoother you are the more power you will develop. Therefore, no matter what effort you put into a shot, you can only develop maximum power if the stroke is smoothly made. The left arm contributes to this.

At your next practice, play several shots of every type of stroke with your left hand in your pocket throughout. Then take it out and consciously make the most use you can of it—without actually playing two-handed, of course— in every one of your strokes. Whatever advantage you gain, build it into your game so that you will perform it naturally. I don't think you'll find that you have altogether wasted your time.

Strokes make the man

Ground strokes, overheads or volleys—your strokes, or a number of them, should be modelled on those of some champion or very good player; otherwise we are admitting that not much is to be learnt from watching such players. But the strokes should be modeled only; naturalness should not be lost. Your strokes may resemble those of another player, but they should not give the impression that you are aping him. Do not copy personal mannerisms; it interferes with your strokes concentration.

In watching champions play, final matches may offer good displays of tactics and exciting finishes, but they are unlikely to provide the best models of stroke-making. Too often the players nullify each other's best shots. To get the most benefit for your own stroke-making repertoire you should watch champions playing in earlier rounds. Here, for instance, with ground strokes, you will see them making time to get behind and over every ball, pause, and then come forward at the ball with a complete mastery over it. You should apply this picture to yourself when playing easy balls. Then, if you try to create opportunities to do so, more and more balls will become easy. Gradually you will get complete mastery over the ball.

It follows that you should have a mental image of what

your own strokes look like. Knowing what a stroke looks like when you play it well will help you to play it well.

Although coaches and champions acknowledge that you should know what you are trying to do in your stroke-production, your strokes are not yet well enough grooved or naturally made if you have to attend to them so much that it distracts you from watching the ball properly. Watching the ball is so important a part of any stroke that nothing should be allowed to interfere with it.

Just as you try to stroke as well as possible, so too should you use your strokes to the best advantage. For instance, never stand there trying to win a rally with beautiful drives from side to side when any one of your drives may be good enough to take you in to the net for an easier volley.

As far as winning a match is concerned, the best time to practice is before it. But, although **practicing** soon after it may seem like locking the stable door after the horse has bolted, it is the best time of all for improving your strokes. With the experience and practice from the match behind you, and any restricting tension removed, you can hit your shots better than ever before, and this becomes your new standard to carry forward to the next match.

Similarly, if you play badly in a match, do not take a rest from the game; practice as soon as possible and regain confidence in your strokes. In this way the periods when you regard yourself as being out of form will be as short as possible and those when you are in form will be as long as possible. People who follow this system have few off-days.

So it turns out that you try to perfect your strokes, practice them before a match, play the match with your strokes as the basis of it, and whether you play well or badly you practice them again. Strokes, strokes, and more strokes. Strokes make the man.

CHAPTER EIGHT

In the face of obstacles

*The right speed/Bad conditions/Disputed points/
Weariness*

Often after you have lost a match you are told you
played the wrong game; that you beat yourself by trying to
hit too hard; that you became overcautious; or that you
made no attempt to lift your game. It is all fairly perplexing,
particularly for juniors, who seem to be accused of trying
to hit the cover off the ball one day and of getting nervous
and playing too tentatively the next.

Perhaps a little advice about *speed* will be acceptable,
so that you can at least play with a clear conscience. Here
are some broad ideas about playing stronger, equal-standard,
and weaker players, together with some points about playing
those retriever-only types.

Stronger opponents. When you are playing out of your
class your opponent will have the initiative practically all
the time, so that you can expect your normal occupation to
consist of chasing his shots from here to there. In such cases
about the only decision to make is whether you will return
everything you can and so get the most play out of the
match, or whether you will hit every bit as hard as your
opponent does and not worry that you cannot expect to
get as many in. Do whichever you feel like on the day.

Playing with a somewhat less than even chance of
winning, it is usually best to play a little faster than normal.
It cannot be helped if a few more errors result. Going along
at your usual speed is likely to bring you defeat, as pre-
dicted.

Evenly matched. With an even chance of winning or losing, either play your own normal game or modify it according to your opponent's type of play. Naturally, if your opponent makes a lot of errors you should give him every chance to continue doing this, by keeping the ball in play. But not too softly, or you will play him into form. If he is a slow player, always keep your speed above his. Do not come down to his speed in an attempt to increase your steadiness. That slow speed is his steadiest speed and it is not likely to be yours. For both these reasons, keep above it.

Weaker players than yourself. It is even more important to stay above your opponent's speed when you are playing someone who people say you should be able to beat. Feeling that you have much to lose and little to gain, it is easy to become very cautious and so drop your game to his. As I see it, this turns the match from odds-on to almost even-money.

Retrievers. If you are playing a man who does nothing but retrieve and hence is good at it, it is almost always bad policy to try to beat him with plain speed. Getting no speed from him, you have to press to generate your own, and as a result you usually beat yourself.* Having few winning shots of his own, this is what he is counting on, fortified by an array of scalps collected from others who have tried to hit him off the court.

The standard tactics against a retriever are to play above his speed, but safely, and to come to the net. Leaving the net aside for a moment, it is not asking too much of yourself to play safely and faster. Your normal safe speed is faster than that of a plain retriever anyway, and it is not as though you have to cope with difficult or penetrating play.

Do not lose your balance and press yourself into error with your ground strokes, and do not rush the net on everything. Take your time and await your many opportunities to

---

* In producing a fast drive it is more difficult to make accurate contact with slow high balls dropping down at a large angle to the path of your racket swing than it is when you are playing against medium-paced shots that come through more in line with your swing.

give him an awkward one and come in to the net. An awkward one can often be a short one, as most retrievers stand well back. Their shots, which are irritatingly high and deep when you are on the baseline, become only high volleys when you are at the net.

Retrievers also lob a lot. Whenever you receive a good lob, do not try to kill it with one smash. It is much safer to have several bites at the apple—until the eventual weak one comes along. In the meantime you are not likely to have the initiative taken away from you by any player who is a confirmed defender.

If you are playing against a man who can play the ball high and deep all day long when you are back and can immediately change to a low, accurate passing shot whenever you come up, then you are not playing a retriever at all—you are up against a really good ground-stroke player. If the general opinion before the match was that you would beat him, then quite obviously you must be a pretty good player and thus well able to look after yourself.

To come back to the pure retriever. Though the accepted tactic against him is to take the net, it may be that this is not your game and that you regard the net position as suicidal. If you have to play him from the baseline it is just as important as before that you keep your speed somewhat above his, because what is natural-speed retrieving for him will be unsafe puddling for you.

You should not regard the retriever as a heart-breaker or a horror player. Unless you have had too much tennis already and are very tired, you should never hate the thought of playing him. If you do you are impatiently worrying too much about that victorious ending of the match. The play is easy enough, and you have the initiative. The match is likely to be long, but why heart-breaking? You should stop building up emotions and play some strokes instead.

For retrievers. If you happen to be a retriever yourself, you probably will always play fairly well and be a reliable and popular man in your own team. You will also be respected as a man who is always hard to beat and who is

Forehand volley easily made, and mind clearly on the game—
a Crawford display of relaxed concentration.
(See text, pages 18, 19)

U.S. L.T.A. photograph

From his right foot Great Britain's Peter Curtis reaches those extra inches. (See text, page 118)

likely to cause upsets in tournaments. But do not expect to win any tournaments in good company. You may upset a few players here and there, but in any one tournament it is too much to expect that all the stroke-players competing will be unsound. If you are a youngish junior do not be over impressed if your completely defensive play gives you comparative success. It is a fair foundation—but only a foundation, so be sure to build some additional structure on it.

For young hard-hitters. If you are a junior who likes hitting hard it is highly likely that this is your most comfortable and natural game. In matches do not bash recklessly or you will be certain to lose and to come in for a lot of criticism, perhaps even contempt, for your play; moreover, no one will want you as a doubles partner. But you should continue to play a fast game, for this is the only way you can move naturally. If you play slowly, your feet will get slow. You will feel clumsier and clumsier, and eventually lose all confidence.

I must have made it clear that I do not recommend slow play and that I do not like it much. I do not admire retrievers-only. I actively dislike tennis that is safety-first-last-and-always—though I do not mind in the least playing against it. Players who pursue the slow-style policy when they have the stroke ability to do far better are really stunting their tennis growth to something like a Japanese pot-plant. Ask yourself what tennis, or life, would be like if no one ever took a risk or showed initiative.

In case you think this amounts to my being all dislikes and nothing else, I will tell you what I do like. I like a smooth stroke-player who fights to the last inch. If he does it coolly as well, then I love him.

Tennis for bad conditions

"I did as well as I could, in the conditions; no one could expect to play properly in *that*," says the disgruntled man who comes off after doing badly in poor conditions and is trying to conceal his chagrin at having lost when on a decent day he thinks he would have won.

A large number of players do not do their best in poor conditions, but would be most offended if anyone told them so. Everyone can play better on a good court on a still day. But, unless you are content to be a fair-weather player, you still have to do your best in bad conditions. You may feel it is not the real game, but the results count just the same. Famous Davis Cup matches have been played in circumstances as bad as we are ever likely to encounter.

In general the best turn you can do yourself is to be prepared in advance for the conditions you must inevitably meet. Make allowance for them instead of merely noting them or going to the extreme of being continually amazed throughout the match whenever anything abnormal happens. Although not expecting to reveal your top form, at least be determined to be put off less than your opponent.

Retaining control in the wind

Recognize the wind's direction in relation to the court, and its strength before you even leave home. For good measure expect it to be stronger again at the courts; if there are a number of them situated in a flat area, it certainly will be. Pilots, always aware in advance of wind conditions, use, say, a crosswind take-off technique from the start; they do not wait to be blown crooked and then make correction. This sort of thing can be applied in tennis. But quite late in a crosswind match you see players hitting balls out down the sideline and obviously feeling that the wind robbed them of the point. Or they play against the wind and hit a lot of balls into the net with the same attitude.

Downwind. When playing downwind (wind behind you) on a strong day, try to hold every game, because the games at this end can become the equivalent of service games. You then try to break one of your opponent's downwind games.

Playing downwind should give you an advantage. The wind gives speed to your strokes without your having to

130

apply it, leaving you free to concentrate more on control. If there is any stroke (except a drop shot, and probably a lob) you would rather play against the wind for safety, it is one of your weaknesses and needs to be given more practice. This is an acid test.

In the meantime, or in any case if the wind is strong, you should modify your strokes to cope with it. Use exaggerated long contact, a shorter and higher backswing, or a little slice, or whatever you like as long as you deliberately *do* something, as distinct from playing some normal shot and blaming the wind for the difference in result. Come to the net a lot more, for the double reason that your approach shots give your opponent less time and that his attempted passing shots will be correspondingly slower.

Upwind. Playing upwind, you may still have to go to the net fairly often. This is one way of stopping the downwind man from having the net all the time. Also, you may find yourself against one of those players who can send a lofted topspin drive deep to the baseline, where it kicks up and carries nearly to the back fence. You will either be forced to deep half-volley a fair number of these or you will have to be at the net. The result of all this is that in a windy match there is likely to be more net play than usual. Playing upwind, do not forget the drop shot.

Crosswind. In a crosswind you normally attack to the side to which the wind is blowing, placing your serve to that side too. This gives your attack more penetration. Playing an awkward or a risky shot or a high lob, you aim for safety and play it towards the cushion of crosswind. Again the net is a good proposition. It is less difficult for you to adjust your volleys in a swinging wind than it is for your opponent to control his passing shots, which have to be made after your approach shots have swung away or in towards his body.

If a diagonal wind is blowing it is a wonderful aid to a downwind swinging service. Left-handers seem to make particularly good use of this.

When two weather-wise merchants play each other in the wind the match is a ding-dong struggle after which it would never occur to anyone to say that no one could possibly play in conditions like that. When one of these men plays a fair-weather opponent in similar conditions he may not actually play as well as he could have on a still day, but he clearly has more chance of walking off the court a winner.

Playing in the wind is a perfect test of whether your tennis attitude is to take every advantage that offers itself or to sit back and receive every blow that fate hands out.

Playing on wet or rough courts

If you are forced to play in the rain you have to decide whether you are more concerned with winning the match or with protecting your racket. You must then concentrate on one of these aims, because you cannot concentrate on both.

Do not fall over two or three times and lose your temper in finding out that the court is slippery. You can expect it to be, particularly if it is grass.

If you have to stop and start again it will not be at match point. Do not imagine that it will be and worry throughout the day. Determine to win the first point when you restart, and let it rest there.

This is easier said than done, but it is about the best you can do. Your opponent may not do even as well.

It's unusual these days to encounter rough hardcourts, but it happens often on grass. Avoid as many bad bounces as possible by going to the net. When you go up on a poor shot you are often saved by a bad bounce interfering with your opponent's intended passing shot.

In playing ground strokes, take them a little later than usual. If you are a firm-wristed player with a well-grooved swing, relax your wrist somewhat so that you can handle any ball that suddenly shoots, kicks up, or changes direction.

Curse the court a bit if you want to, but never so much that it takes up the attention you should be giving to coping.

Handling doubtful decisions

A small book could be written about disputed line decisions on vital points and resulting upsets and "incidents," backed with its author's reasoning on why all sorts of cases occurred and exactly how each one should have been dealt with. But it would probably leave you unconvinced and would certainly bore you. I propose to substitute a condensed account of likely situations and a suggested line of conduct.

"Incidents" on a tennis court are thoroughly deplorable. Never create one, and always do your level best not to be involved in one.

Whenever you feel upset about anything—and the most usual cause is a line decision against you—the golden rule of experience is to lose that point only and never a string of them as a sort of angry or dejected reaction.

When playing without an umpire you call the shots at your end and your opponent calls them at his. Make it a point of pride that you never deliberately call a shot wrongly. I am not preaching. You are sure to find that the self-respect this policy brings you is a most sustaining asset in your play.

If you play on after a doubtful ball and eventually lose the rally you cannot go back and say that the earlier ball was out. To do so would mean that you were playing with no chance of losing whereas your opponent might be exhausting himself in the rally. This is a code rather than a rule and if you break it you will almost certainly bring yourself into contempt. Just the same, the safest thing with doubtful balls is always to play on. Most doubtful balls actually touch the line, and you are not being honest either to yourself or to your opponent if you call for a let on a ball that was really in, just because you were momentarily in doubt about it. An important and overall point to remember is that the policy of playing on prevents you from being hesitant and from watching the line hopefully instead of the ball intently.

In other words, it is not as naïve as you may have thought. You will be chivalrous, but not to your own disadvantage.

When you have an umpire, play to his calls and pay no attention to where the ball goes in relation to the line. Query only what may be a blatant error. If you receive a point you should not have received on some close ball, never try to even things up by giving away the next point. If your opponent were to do the same thing you would be like a couple of accountants balancing the books, the spectators would be mumbling, and the umpire would be entitled to walk off. Remember that you are playing to the umpire's call and not to where the ball lands. Leave any possible evening-up to the umpire.

You will be wise to expect a mistake or two from an umpire. However good he is, there will be times when he cannot see the ball as well as the players can, and he lacks their instinctive judgment of whether a close ball is likely to be in or out before it lands. In top-class games where officials take every precaution, errors still occur. Take, for example, those games where there is a man for every line. This system would be foolproof except that with so many linesmen there is all the more chance for one of them to lapse. The whole arrangement has long reminded me of those early twin-engined airplanes that could not fly on one engine. Instead of increasing safety they doubled the chance of an engine failure.

We are all far more critical than logical about umpiring mistakes. We take hundreds of correct decisions for granted, and when a couple of bad ones come along we enlarge their importance and forget that in most matches they are pretty evenly distributed.

It is reasonable to say that umpires are nearly always fair but seldom impartial. There is a vast difference between these two states of mind. All of us tend to see things as we want to see them. An experienced umpire knows this and overcomes his partialities. An inexperienced umpire does not know it and "calls the balls as he sees them," to the anguish of the victimized side. This is exactly what happens in lower-grade and junior-team finals, where the player/umpires are most inexperienced and where most discontent occurs. But no one is being deliberately unfair.

Wrongs that don't make rights

Nor does cheating abound in non-umpired matches in any particular tournament or district. Onlookers, in the throes of anxiety, are certain that they are constantly seeing examples, but few players can say they have been deliberately and consistently cheated throughout a match.

Hard-court players, from long association with ball marks just touching the edges of lines, become accustomed to very deep shots being in and the rally continuing. In their first grass-court tournament they often get quite a shock, while their supporters become indignant and may roundly declare the whole tournament fit for outlaws only. Without ball marks—which are a very mixed blessing when the lines themselves are not perfect—players call the balls as they see them, and most very close balls do appear to be out. Add to this that little extra for biased hopefulness previously attributed to umpires, and most certainly they will look to be out. After playing on grass for a while the hard-court players themselves see things the same way. If you understand this in advance you will not become upset as dozens of players before you have allowed themselves to be.

Do not imagine that people who deliberately cheat gain an overall advantage. They sneak an extra point here and there, but the attached disadvantages are heavy. If they are not good at cheating they alert their opponent at once, and this mostly tends to harden his determination and make him concentrate on hitting the ball well in. No matter how good cheats are, they always become known, and eventual humiliation awaits them. Anyone so good at cheating that he would never be pinned down would be wasting his time at tennis. He should be busily engaged in cheating at cards and making himself a fortune.

Retaliation is not the best answer to cheating. It only

involves you in it yourself. The best counter, as I have already said, is increased determination and concentration, backed by the resolve that, come what may, you will lose only the point concerned and no more in sympathy with it.

Just as distant fields look greener, so too does a point you were unfairly deprived of. It would have meant game, perhaps, and that would have meant a score of such-and-such, and so on, till eventually a lost match becomes attributable to one point. Maybe it was, and I don't propose to argue it back and forth and end by not convincing anyone who does not want to be convinced.

The distastrous turn of the tide hinging on one point—and that point, by long, long coincidence, a disputed one—happens incomparably more often to juniors and inexperienced players than it does to hardened competitors. Therefore there must be more to it than the actual point alone.

Take it or leave it, the essence of being able to look after yourself in any company and at any age or grade lies in your being able to give everything you've got to the next point, the one that is coming up, no matter what happened to the last one. I think most match-toughened people will agree.

Serving into the sun

At Wimbledon, unlike Australia, they do not have to serve into the morning sun. When a player is invited to compete in the Gentlemen's Singles Championship he is not expected to get out of bed in the morning to do so. The earliest matches are programmed for two o'clock in the afternoon, after everyone has had a good lunch.

Like most other things, this procedure has a catch or two in it. Sometimes the late starters have to battle it out in the long twilight, and then they have a very late dinner indeed. In the 1930's the great Jack Crawford gave one of his most beautiful displays late one afternoon and evening. Queen Mary sat enthralled in the Royal Box until eight o'clock, and the maestro was described in the London papers as the

Julie Heldman is oblivious to the mud. (See text, page 132)

U.S. L.T.A. photograph

Rosewall's left foot will not cross beyond his right, and this forehand will be played along the front leg. (See text, page 116)

man who kept Her Majesty waiting for the royal meal. The important catch is that they still have to serve into the sun. Baffling as it may seem to all God-fearing sons of the Southern Hemisphere, in the Northern Hemisphere it is the right-handers who have to serve into the afternoon sun.

About 1907 there were very few left-handers about. This was due to the prevailing barbaric practice of training practically all natural left-handers shortly after birth into awkward and sometimes stammering right-handers. However, in 1907 the Wimbledon title was won by a left-hander, the Australian Norman Brookes. One newspaper reporter, forgetting that he was supposed to be a sporting writer, wrote that Brookes had had an unfair advantage since, being left-handed, he did not have to serve looking into the sun. This observation was justly considered a bad show indeed because it was directed against a visitor to England. A local player was always fair game for the Press, but a visitor could do no wrong, even by playing with his left hand. Wimbledon felt suitably mortified.

When we start at 8.30 a.m. (will English readers please stop shuddering?) we Southern Hemisphere right-handers must not feel too sorry for ourselves. We are not the only people who have to serve bang into the sun. As you will have gathered, Crawford had to for at least some of the time he was enthralling Her Majesty. Brookes' right-handed opponents did the same thing one by one, and as long as there's a Wimbledon and afternoon sunshine in an English July it will remain so.

There is nothing to serving into the sun—except for the trying fact that you cannot produce your normal serve. Whenever your normal throw puts the ball in line with the sun it is wrong to grit your teeth and screw up your eyes and go ahead with it anyhow. It tends to blind you for the return, and that's poor tennis.

A better alternative, with the sun in a really bad position, is to alter your throw (and hence your action, and to some extent the effectiveness of your serve) so that you do not throw the ball directly in line with the sun and you can therefore see the return clearly. Somewhere between your left shoulder and well over to your right-hand side there is a place where you can throw the ball so that it will not be in line with the sun. The difference between this and your normal throw can be lessened by finding the best place to stand between center-mark and sideline. You should also slightly alter, in one direction or the other, your normal side-on position to the net. The result of all this is that for every hour of the morning, you can avoid serving directly into the sun. You do not need a wide-brimmed hat or anything else of the sort.

If you see your opponent serving hard and strong with exactly the same throw and action he used at the good end, you can be sure that he is looking into the sun and chancing that his serve alone will be good enough to beat you. So do not go for too much on your return of service and give him a fifty-fifty chance by risking an error. Get it back into play; even if it is a bit weak it is on the way to a man who will not see it as well as he would like to.

And you need not worry about your English cousins and their visitors serving endlessly on end into the sun for as long as there's a Wimbledon and for as long as right-handers continue to dominate the earth. They will not be looking into the sun. If they were inexperienced enough to do so, they could be as gentlemanly as they liked, but they would never be invited to play in the Gentlemen's Singles at Wimbledon. They would not be good enough to attract the playing public. Beneath the buttoned coat of the English official may beat a generous heart, but beneath his bowler hat there also ticks a very hard head.

Weary, but a winner

Everyone has to play some of his matches when he is tired. No matter how fit you are, occasions will arise when the difference between winning and losing depends chiefly on your remaining energy.

Guard against *mental lethargy*. When tired you are often

rather relaxed and become too easily satisfied with something less than your best. You feel you have done well to get as far as this, you are hitting the ball smoothly from the center of your strings, you are far from disgracing yourself . . . and after all you will not really mind if you lose.

Don't worry, you will lose all right, unless the other man happens to be an even greater sleepwalker than you are. Anyway, very soon afterwards, when you have had a refreshing shower, you will feel highly dissatisfied. You must therefore divorce physical tiredness from mental lethargy, and this is best done by having some constructive ideas to put into practice.

If your opponent has had as many matches as you have, he will be equally tired. Be fully conscious of this. If anyone is going to relax contentedly, let it be him.

Avoid serving two balls as much as possible. Until you have tried this you can have no idea how much effort (physical on the first serve, mental on the second) it can save you. Just slip the first ball in; if he is tired he will not do a great deal to it.

As soon as you give your opponent a shot that is a little awkward for him, don't be hesitant about following it in to the net. It shortens the rallies, and running forward is less tiring than running from side to side.

Always keep the rallies short—unless, of course, you keep them long deliberately because you feel this is even more weakening for him than for you. Break up any rally that is developing badly by going for a fast shot or a drop-shot, or alter it by hoisting a high lob. Whatever you do, don't stagger from side to side like a puppet on a string, slowly but surely losing the point. It is all too likely to cost you the next one as well.

When you have to smash, even if it is not a difficult shot, keep yourself compact. When tired, never give your solar-plexus muscles a bad stretching; if you do, it will weaken you severely.

When you are just keeping the ball going, remember that the ground strokes that take the least effort are the straight forehand and the cross-court backhand. More concentration, wrist effort and shoulder-turning are required for their opposite numbers, which also have a tendency to be short when you are tired. It is just too bad if you are playing a left-hander; this is another of the natural advantages left-handers have.

There will probably be a lot of sweat about, but it can only do you much harm if it gets in your eyes. Use a damp towel instead of carelessly dashing handfuls of water into your face.

One last word, before medical men or worried wives descend on me. If you are well over forty, somewhat too fat, and really distressed, forfeit. Tell your opponent he was too good. He will not feel deprived of anything. Fighting on till the last gasp is a fine thing to encourage in all young sportsmen, but for some of older vintage it might turn out to be literally true.

If you find an equally tired opponent who knows everything I have put down here, then clearly both of you are in for an exhausting time. If he does not know it, you have a better chance of beating him than if you were both fresh. Who would have thought it?

CHAPTER NINE

Effective doubles

Tactics and position / Serving ends and receiving sides

Long rallies, with the advantage changing from one side to the other and back again; baseline and net attack equally shared during a game; fluctuating fortunes with service games being won and lost—these variations are part and parcel of singles matches up to a quite high-grade of tennis, after which, unfortunately, they are seldom seen. They do not belong to doubles.

It could be said that top-class singles, at its present stage, is played more like a doubles match with only one man on each side. The net is always the best position, if it can be covered. Present-day champions can cover it better than it was ever covered before, by a combination of more consistently effective serving and greater speed about the court. Human measurements have steadily increased while court dimensions have remained static. Another reason advanced is that the standard of present-day ground strokes has deteriorated by about as much as serving and net-play have improved; this is not true of the best champions, but unfortunately it applies to much of the championship play we see.

The result has been that top-class singles has gone down in value as a spectator attraction. Various amendments to the rules have been suggested: that only one service attempt be allowed (but this would take excitement and power from the game and would mar any lesser grade of tennis by causing too many double-fault equivalents); that the serve be made from a line marked one yard behind the existing baseline (amongst other objections, this would hamper the development of juniors); that the server be barred from volleying until after the first return of service has been made (tried by professionals, without generating enthusiasm in anyone). The best solution would seem to be to lower the compression of the balls. This, without all the fuss of altering thousands of courts throughout the world, would have the same effect as making the court larger or of lowering the net height a little. In top-class singles the required balance between ground strokes and net play would be restored, and everyone else would find it easier to hit the ball in. Everyone? Yes, everyone. Perhaps there lies the rub. Would ladies' singles ever finish?

Now back to our game of doubles, which is just starting.

Doubles has distinct tactics of its own, its association with singles play disappearing relatively early in competitive tennis. From this point doubles becomes more a matter of taking what you can whenever you can. A pair who know their business create their opportunities rather than wait for them to occur, and this chapter deals only with this advanced form of doubles play.

To all intents and purposes, having the net means having the advantage. As the serving side has the first opportunity to get both players to the net, it works out in a contest between two good doubles pairs that without fail all four players follow their services to the net. The serving side wins most of the games; not so much because the serves are greatly superior to the returns as because the serving side consistently has first use of the net by both players.

Championship doubles matches vary widely, sometimes producing the best exhibition of the art, and sometimes a most boring display of it. Tactics in either case consist of the players making virtually certain of holding their service games (so that the set cannot be lost) and of attacking so strongly with returns of service that almost any risk is justifiable if the result is that any one of the opponents' service games is broken. When the ground strokes are good the spectacle, fittingly, is top-class; when they are not, long but unexciting advantage sets are likely to result from the hit-and-miss tennis of the receivers.

Once away from the unhappy combination of top-class serving and inadequate ground strokes, doubles again becomes a balanced and interesting game. Lesser lights, while still striving to follow the same top-class tactics, are less certain of holding their services; consequently they try harder to break all their opponents' service games. This means that, though still attacking with their service returns, they try for fewer all-or-nothing shots and do not easily give up any game that may have begun badly for them.

Whatever other assets a doubles pair may have, to be consistently successful they must develop the following mixed bag of attributes: ability to place their second service as well as their first; determination to be at the net at every opportunity; ability to cover the net; ability to play rolled rising-ball returns of service from either court; and determination in each player to play with his partner at all times during a match and never desert him or play against him.

Whatever the standard of the two players' strokes, here is a system for using them to very great effect.

Service principles in doubles

The players serve as a pair, and win or lose each service game that way. If one man is not serving well, the net-man must cover the centre as actively as ever, even if it means risking his own sideline rather more than usual. A pair is at its weakest if the server is left to sink or swim.

The server normally serves to the backhand, unless the receiver is definitely weak (as distinct from erratic) on the forehand. Even though some players' backhands might be their steadier stroke, backhands usually have less speed and topspin dip on them and are easier to volley. When serving, you are not after a fifty-fifty chance of the receiver's beating you or making an error; you are after the highest possible odds of being able to put your first volley in and deep, after which the odds on your winning the point immediately rise steeply. If the first serve misses, it is more important again that the second one should be to the backhand.

Doubles statistics show that many more serving points are won from first serves than from second ones. This supports what experienced doubles players know already—namely, that it is essential to get a large number of your first serves in rather than serve too ambitiously and miss too many. It does not mean that you should serve your first ball so slowly that the opponents never need to guard against a threatened ace and can always stand well in and treat it as a second serve.

The normal means adopted by servers to get a lot of first balls in while remaining potentially dangerous is to use a form of American-twist serve for doubles. Not the exaggerated type, where the ball is thrown well over the left shoulder and is all kick and no speed, but one where the ball is thrown over the head and carries enough topspin to allow it to go well over the net and yet drop into court.

Service to the first court

The first-court serve to the receiver's backhand takes a lot of practice, but it pays large dividends. Few people can make a backhand return from this side that is damaging to a serving opponent of about their own standard. If the first serve goes in, the reply is often a toss, which is just what the net-man should be waiting for; and even the second serve will command respect.

You can achieve this center-line service by three different methods: stand near the center-mark and serve straight down the center; stand nearly halfway out to the sideline and serve over the second-court side of the net-band so that your service swerves into the first court near the center-line; stand well out towards the sideline, forcing the receiver to move out to cover a threatened ace wide of his forehand and uncover a fairly wide amount of backhand court.

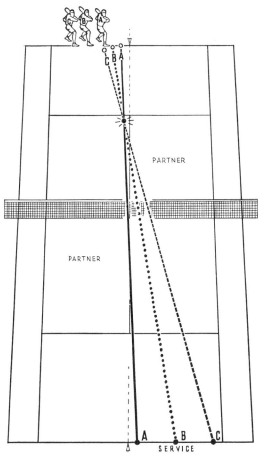

THREE WAYS OF SERVING TO FIRST-COURT RECEIVER'S BACKHAND

A-A: Stand near center-mark and serve down receiver's center-line.

B-B: Server's position forces receiver to stand farther out; but a sliced serve must be aimed to the right of the center band.

C-C: Server's position threatens an ace, forcing receiver to uncover a fair amount of backhand space.

147

The odd wide serve to the forehand should be mixed in, for it is quite effective even without much pace against a man who up till then has been consistently forced to use his backhand. Against players who are hoping to step round your second serve you will often find you can get more slow, swerving second-service aces than any other type.

What is really bad tactics is to aim your first serve to your first-court opponent's forehand line and miss it, then feel no confidence in being able to land in either a second very wide one or one to his backhand. You then usually send over a nondescript second serve which he plays most confidently with his forehand, leaving you with perhaps a less than fifty-fifty chance with your first volley. Bad tactics indeed, particularly if you have served from near the center-mark, but you see it done countless times.

For most servers the first court is the danger side, there being always the possibility of losing the point against a good forehand return of service. or of double-faulting in trying to avoid the receiver's forehand. It is also a fact that many pairs often lack concentration on the first point of the game.

Service to the second court

It is easier to find the receiver's backhand in the second court, and if you can hold the points in the first court you will usually handle the other side well enough. Provided, of course, that you can guard against that fatal lack of concentration which can occur in doubles when the server is ahead by one point. In this connection you should also be aware of the so-called "sucker shot." This is where the receiver gives you a high forehand first volley and in trying to sideline the first-court net-man with it you slice it out the sideline. There is nothing wrong with this shot if it goes in; it has gained its name from the number of times it has been responsible for converting a winning position into a lost point.

What if you strike a left-hander in the second court? If

you see in the hit-up that he is one of those with a very good forehand it is best not to experiment but to shut this dangerous shot out of the game from the very start. Play tandem (which as a pair you should have practiced) from the first ball you serve to him. To do this stand right up to the center-mark, throw the ball over your right shoulder and swerve it down the centre-line. To cover the extra court that you will have to leave open, your partner has to stand nearer the center and a little farther back than usual, and he has to stay well awake if you want your opening tandem attempt to be successful. The left-hander's natural doubles backhand is to its off—that is, towards your tandem partner, and the left-hander will most likely try to toss over your partner or play a short underspin shot wide of his backhand volley into the extra space he had to leave in moving his own net position nearer the center to suit your tandem serve. As it never pays to play to a net-man who is waiting for you, the left-hander will soon be forced to turn his backhand-cut service return round to your side; you will then have the easier task of making your first volley against this shot instead of against the wide dipping forehand you would have to meet if you had not played tandem. Vary the tandem, however, and return to the orthodox formation now and then. Playing tandem means there is no net-man directly opposite the receiver, and with this threat permanently removed any receiver will sooner or later begin to feel comfortable.

What if the left-hander, as well as having a good fore-hand, has a good rolled cross-court backhand and is capable of pulling your tandem center-line serve wide of your over exposed forehand volley? Well, even though you and your partner will have seen in the hit-up the type of left-hander he is and his style of play, it is probably still worth opening with tandem to find out if he really has that shot which so few left-handers have when the game is actually on. If he has, and it is too good for the exposed forehand side of yours which the tandem leaves, then you will have to go back to the safer cover of the orthodox formation and cope

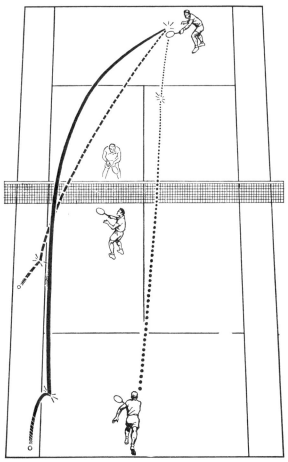

TANDEM AGAINST A LEFT-HANDER

When first confronted with the tandem formation and a service to his backhand, a left-hander is likely to continue hitting his return in its usual direction. As this means either sidelining the tandem net-man, or lobbing over him, the net-man must be every bit as alert as the server.

with his returns of service as best you can. This can't be helped. It seems to be another fact of life that a good left-hander is a very good doubles player.

So far you have only got your serve in. You have not even made your first volley. I'm sorry if you feel this is too detailed, but I can assure you that some of your future opponents will have this knowledge, some of them well before they are eligible to vote. If you do not have it too, then any pair of them will be too solid for you and any partner you care to choose, although their singles strokes may be no stronger. Any system of using your strokes in doubles, unless detailed, will be so full of holes as to be useless and confusing in match play.

The high premium on first volleys

Serve with the necessary rhythm or balance that allows you to follow in to the net without any break, come right in, pause, volley deep to someone's backhand (which is always possible if both your opponents have stayed back), and wait for the almost certain toss. If it is a good one, you or your partner should go back a few steps and smash it at half to three-quarter pace well over the net. For choice it should go either down the middle towards the first-court player's backhand or else to the second-court player's backhand, the aim being to provoke another toss. You do this till the short one comes along, and then you know what to do—and the harder the better.

Players who realize the importance of the first volley rarely miss it. They do everything possible to prevent it from being difficult, and when it is they try to scramble it back in any fashion but at all costs. If it is sufficiently manageable to allow them to play it deep, they know that the odds on their winning the rally are high and they do not lightly throw them away. If you yourself have not realized the importance of the first volley before, you should watch how it is approached by leading players. You may see some hit-and-miss on other strokes, particularly on service-return, but you'll see very little on the first volley.

The distance you come in to the net after your serve is as far as you can get, allowing for the fractional pause you need before volleying. You cannot volley with control while you are on the run, any more than you can stretch as wide as when you are stationary.

The net-man's cover

You have now done as much as you can to make the first volley easy. It will clearly be all the easier if you have to make it only on the sideline side, either right or left, depending on which side you are serving to, without having to worry about the middle as well. This is where the net-man comes in. He should be able to cover as far across as the center-line and thus protect the middle for the server, so that as often as possible only the sideline volley has to be played. The net–man has also to ensure that no lob ever gets over his head.

In fulfilling these two responsibilities the net-man can stand wherever he likes—but he must fulfill them. You will see at a glance that it would be useless for him to stand right over on the sideline and close up to the net looking like a damsel in distress in mixed doubles. On further reflection you will probably agree that most people stand too close to the net and also that even if they stand well away from the sideline they do little, beyond an occasional death-or-glory interception, to really cover the middle for their partners. In quite a lot of advanced doubles play the net-man does too little.

The most probable reason for the incorrect positioning and inadequate participation of net players is that they have seen where the champions stand and have followed suit without realizing the difference in circumstances. Champion players, because of their extra speed of reflex and movement, anticipation, etc., can cover both the middle volley and any lob attempted over their heads from a closer net position

Damsel, but seldom in distress: Kerry Melville. (See text, page 152)

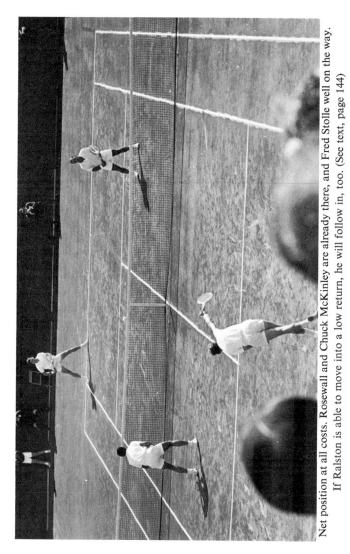

Net position at all costs. Rosewall and Chuck McKinley are already there, and Fred Stolle well on the way. If Ralston is able to move into a low return, he will follow in, too. (See text, page 144)

than the rest of us; they can therefore stand closer for greater severity and still cover what they have to.

The average advanced player has to stand a little farther back if he is to achieve the same cover. But not too far back. If he goes too far back the receiver will attack him instead of the incoming server, who will have come right up and past him. In short, since you must be at the net in doubles, then in your efforts to cover it you must not leave it by so much that your position changes from attacking to defensive. Your position has to be such that you can step forward to volley and move quickly backwards to cover lobs on the full.

The net-man, covering as far as the center-line, should volley every return of service that he possibly can. Before the server can volley, he has to follow in fast to gain his net position; he also needs to steady himself by means of that fractional pause. The net-man is already in position and already steadied.

The average net-man does not make sufficient use of his advantages and takes far too few service returns. This again may be due to what is seen in top championship doubles and adopted for the wrong reason. The champions are so well aware of the net-man's advantages that they direct their service returns far enough away from him to keep him out of the game at this vital return-of-service stage. In lower grade doubles plenty of service returns are there for the taking; the net-man simply does not move over and take them.

Above all, the net-man must never allow a toss to get over his head.

Blanketing the net

From the description given so far you may have noticed that in their tactics to hold service the serving pair have got everything nicely blocked off, except for two possible shots. One is the lob over the incoming server's head, the other is the passing shot down the net-man's sideline.

Neither stroke is a percentage shot for the receiver, and

if you watch a championship doubles you will see how rarely either is attempted. To convince yourself that neither stroke pays, you and your partner should try them when you are receiving in a practice set. The lob over the server's head is very seldom open to you. The shot past the net-man is spectacular when successful, but, all told, you usually lose more of them than you win.

The net-man has to watch his sideline when his partner has served wide, and he must watch it if the opposing receiver is clearly gunning for him; but he must not be so over concerned with it that he fails to protect the center. If he looks after his own sideline, lets his partner try to cope with both center and the outside sideline, merely crosses over when lobbed over, and later tells either himself or his friends that the match was lost because his partner kept on losing his serve, then, to put it mildly, he is not playing with his partner—so he is breaking one of the imperatives I quoted at the start of this section.

Whatever his serve is like, the server must come to the net. If it is strong, he comes in to take full advantage. If it is weak, he simply cannot afford not to come in, otherwise it can be returned with complete certainty and his opponents will have the net position.

Breaking your opponent's service

We now leave the serving pair and turn to the matter of breaking your opponents' service games. This also is achieved by gaining the net position. You try to play your own service games with no ground strokes at all. In receiving, the ideal tactics would be to play only one ground stroke, the necessary return of service.

As an example of how to apply these tactics, we will assume that you are starting a match against a pair whose play is unknown to you. It is your opponents' serve, and one of them is going to serve to you in the first court. Your partner stands at the net, or close enough to move in a little as you hit the return, so that you have one man up already.

If the server does not follow his serve to the net, then play it back to him, without taking the smallest risk of missing it, and follow in to the net where the odds are at once in your favor. If the server does follow in, and his partner is standing too close to the net, then, making sure your toss is not a feeble one, put the ball over the net-man's head and come in. This opening is available more often than many players think, especially from the first court, where the shot can usually be played from your forehand over the net-man's backhand side.

Play this shot every time the opportunity is there, no matter how many times, even consecutively. It is easy to make, and it is most penetrating. When this type of net-man finally gets himself set to protect it, he usually leaves you the middle to drive into, and perhaps even straight through.

It sounds easy, but doubles in such conditions, unless the server serves very well indeed, is hardly more than that.

It is only where the server consistently comes in and his partner covers both lobs and the center that you are forced into playing some real doubles. Try to play a rolled rising-ball cross-court shot as quickly and as low over the net as possible and dipping below it, and if you have managed to keep in balance as well you should follow in behind it. If the server is going to have his first volley, this is the most difficult one you can force on him.

There are variations, of course, such as very low and slow returns which catch the incoming server right at his feet, but if you base your service returns on taking the ball late or always slicing it—usually a little too high—his first volleys will be much easier to make.

Cover your own overheads

You have already seen how vital it is that, whenever you and your partner have the net, serving or receiving, no toss should ever get over your heads. So that each player will be constantly alert to this, each must be primarily responsible for any ball he does allow to get over him.

157

It may be argued that it is easier for a man to recover his partner's mistake because he can run diagonally, whereas the other man has to turn round and run straight back. That is quite true, but against good pairs you mostly lose the point anyway whenever one player lets the side down by allowing a lob to get over his head. It therefore pays not to divide up the responsibility and instead to have each player completely responsible for handling every toss on his side of the court. This does not prevent either partner from chasing the other's odd mistakes when he is in a position to do so.

Smash to the backhand, usually, when your opponents are back, but, if either is at the net, avoid smashing straight into that already prepared waist-high backhand volley. This warning applies also to rapid net exchanges. Close to his right side, especially near his waist, a man rarely has a volley at all until he moves his body out of the way.

Playing against your partner

You may remember that determination never to do this is one of the attributes of a good pair. But how, you may ask, could such an apparently improbable thing happen anyway? It happens under tension, and partners who are relatives are rather prone to it.

Imagine that you have worked very hard, say, for a set in hand and four-three in the second and it is your serve. Again you put everything you have into it and reach 40-30. One point to go for five-three. Then, to take the worst case I can think of, your partner lets himself get lobbed over, not once but twice, twice running, to reverse the score to advantage-receiver. This is the kind of abrupt change that affects the nerve of almost any player. Suddenly made reckless, you crack your first serve very hard, only to find it given out by a fraction. Convinced that the whole unhappy situation is the fault of your blundering partner who deserves a lesson, or that it is hardly any concern of yours any longer anyhow, you then serve an angry or exasperated double-fault.

This is a most provocative example, but it still amounts

to playing against your partner, and I think it shows why, in describing this attribute, I use the word *determination*. There are many less provocative situations in which partners can be tempted into playing against each other. Such behavior cannot be dismissed as childish, because so many men even of steady nature slip into it now and then. I would be prepared to call it human. I also think it well worth knowing about and guarding against.

Signals

Are signals made by the net-man behind his back to his serving partner the last word in doubles combination?

Perhaps, but only when the server is accurate enough to meet the signal with exactly the right service. Otherwise the net-man could go the wrong way for the serve that actually results, or he could even be left diving all over the place in perfect time, but uselessly, on a serve that is a fault. Also, your partner could give you a signal for a wide serve just as you were concentrating on a center one and working out exactly where you were going to be for your first volley. This could well make you feel that he had interfered and that the responsibility for the point was now his and not yours. You would then be heading straight towards playing against your partner.

As a general rule, I'd say that it's better to play to your established system with each man looking after his own responsibilities than to place much faith in impromptu signals for one quick coup. But no doubt, as ever with artists at the top of the tree, it is different with the champions.

Choosing correct court sides

Which side of the court should you and your various partners take? There is quite a lot to this question.

With *two right-handers,* the first court is taken by the stronger forehand, the second by the better backhand. It is a mistake to have your strength to the center where, you may reason, most shots are directed by your opponents. Your outside wings are the most easily reached by your opponents' services, so you would be making your opponents a virtual present of your own and your partner's weaker sides.

If one partner is the stronger on both forehand and backhand, then he is almost invariably the stronger player all round and should normally go to the second court, where he can take more of the game. Having read earlier that the first court is the danger court for the server, you may think it should follow that the first court is exactly where the stronger player should be—for maximum devastation, as it were. In exceptional cases this could be the correct procedure, but not as a general rule. In mixed doubles, to take an extreme example of difference in strengths between the two partners, a man taking the first court almost puts himself out of the game.

An old idea was that the first court should be taken by the driver and the second by the volleyer. If this concept of doubles is still used in the grade in which you are playing, then it is as correct as it ever was. Perhaps I am being too hard there. It is logical and it is correct. It applies to mixed doubles. It is just that I should not like to leave any improving and competent net pair with the wrong idea that a man who drives well should not come to the net and play volleys whenever he can.

The first court is the easier side for a beginner because it is the forehand court. Once players can make a backhand adequately, the second court becomes the easier court. For this reason it is taken by the stronger player so that he can make the most use of it. As well as being able to cover (including overhead) more of the court in general once the return of service is made, he can also make better use of his service returns. He is attacking the server's backhand, and with his most easily produced strokes as well (namely, his straight forehand and crosscourt backhand).

Any idea of putting the weaker player on the easier side to make it easier for him is negative thinking instead of positive when taking the two players as a pair. As well, the weaker player's backhand may not be quite up to the constant attention it is likely to get in the second court.

Specializing on first or second court?

Should you, as an individual player and not as part of a pair, specialize on one side? I don't think so. If you have strokes that will go only one way you will have to play on one side only, otherwise the difference in your effectiveness will be so great that by playing on the wrong side you will really be giving your opponents a handicap start. Specializing on one side in doubles tends to type your strokes for singles, and this, since it greatly aids your opponent's anticipation, is bad. It is best to be fully effective on either side.

If you must specialize, you are fortunate if your preference is for the first court. You will become a popular and perhaps even sought-after doubles partner, because almost as many players prefer the second court as call "rough" when you spin your racket for service.

A regular pair should work out their sides and normally never change from them.

Which is the left-hander's side? Though they are complicating my book, I must admit I have always liked left-handers. They provide an interesting variation to the game. When balanced, their style is attractive to watch. Two of them played both singles matches for Australia in a fairly recent Davis Cup success, and four have won Wimbledon. They seem to be increasing in numbers, so perhaps one day we may have famous doubles pairs of left-handers. In the meantime, pairs containing one left-hander are common enough to merit consideration.

The left-hander is not as welcome a doubles partner as he once was. In past days he was more of an unsettling rarity to the opposition, and to partner him there used to be more players whose doubles game was based on strong cross-court forehand driving from the first court and little else. With all the volleyers about now, and with the overwhelming preference for the second court, the left-hander, instead of being welcome, is often *de trop*. Nevertheless, where should he go?

To the second court. It is here that he is the greatest worry to the opposing server. His cross-court forehand is often the best shot on the court, and his backhand is difficult to find. As mentioned earlier, left-handers are most adept at covering their backhands and often play their best forehand of all when stepping round it. Right-handed servers so seldom practice serving down the second-court center-line that when they want to do it in a doubles match against a left-hander they are rarely accurate enough. It was for these reasons that I suggested playing tandem against them, although it is an awkward and uncomfortable formation for the serving pair and concedes that the left-hander is too good in the orthodox way.

You might be tempted to say that where a right-hander and left-hander both have steadier backhands than forehands they should play on opposite sides. They should do so only if either's forehand is so bad that it has to be concealed at all costs, or if they are playing against opponents who are not particularly net-conscious. When a player's backhand is steadier than his forehand it is usually a slice. Where the opponents do not consistently follow their services to the net, the left- and right-handers, playing from their normally wrong sides, can slice their backhand service returns steadily back into play and take the net. If the servers are consistent net players, however, you will have seen from the earlier description of systematic doubles play that they will not mind these steady slices. They will be quite content to make the easy, long, diagonal service to the corners—that is, to the left-hander's backhand in the first court and to the right-hander's backhand in the second court—and to come in for a safe first volley with its accompanying odds-on success. Defeat for the criss-crossed left- and right-handed pair should be almost inevitable as soon as they lose one of their own services.

Finally, you may wish to know what is the best formation for a balanced right-hander and a balanced left-hander because you feel there is a strong case for their playing in the opposite courts. You say that both volley well and could therefore intercept well; that both smash well, and could therefore cover the center well instead of having two backhands to deal with lobs down-center; and that both have balanced ground strokes and would therefore each rather play straight forehands and cross-court backhands. Surely, then, they should play on the opposite sides? Why, it even begins to look like being the best possible doubles combination that could be chosen.

Again the answer, in general, is no. And if you add, as one last ounce to tip the scales, that they both have rolled backhands, the answer in general is still no. If they are balanced players, their forehands are likely to be their stronger and certainly their more dangerous sides. The server would prefer to serve to their backhands and, as I have said before, there is nothing a server likes better than serving his easily made diagonal serves to the backhands of left- and right-handers playing in the wrong courts. Against net-conscious servers a receiving pair should always take up whatever is their most dangerous attacking formation.

At the thoroughly net-conscious standard of doubles a left-hander should be in the first court only if he has a backhand so much more dangerous than his forehand that it is faster and carries more topspin and he himself definitely prefers it to his forehand. When such unusual conditions apply, you really have the basis for an exceptional doubles pair. One of the most famous doubles pairs of all time—John Bromwich and Adrian Quist—was constituted in this way. Bromwich's ground strokes and volleys were made as a left-hander, consisting of a left-handed forehand and a two-handed backhand. At least that is how I regarded them, and those who saw him play may remember that when forced wide on his two-handed side he always used a single-handed left-handed backhand and not a right-handed forehand.

In this Bromwich-Quist pairing we had the left-hander with the exceptional backhand playing in the first court—and we therefore had our exceptional pair. I hope you are sporting enough to admit that I had to find an exceptional man, plus a backhand that was exceptional enough to be two-handed, before I could make your case hold good. And while we're talking in superlatives I think we may as well take a moment off, even though it is not exactly relevant, to pay tribute to Quist as an exceptionally fine second-court doubles player.

Opening service in doubles

The question who should serve first and from which end can fortunately be covered by a shorter answer.

A pair should decide which is its stronger service game. This is normally where the stronger server is doing the serving. But not necessarily. Remember that you win or lose each service as a pair.

When you have choice of ends, or when each partner is content to serve from either end, you should always open with your stronger service game. This ensures your playing at least as many service games that way, if not more, than with your weaker formation.

Starting with your weaker formation (perhaps with some idea of not gambling with the stronger one at the start) can unnecessarily cost you the set. Your opponents start with their stronger serve and win; you follow with your weaker serve and lose, making the score two-love against you; you then break their weaker serve and hold your stronger one to draw level; if this pattern continues you will lose 4-6. And yet it is often unthinkingly followed.

Each set being a separate entity, you can use your stronger service game last in one set and begin with it again in the next set. You should always do this when there is to be no change of serving end for each partner or when a change of end is of no consequence to either partner.

Opening from the most suitable end

When you do not have the choice of end, either in the first set or in any following one, conditions of sun and wind may make it more important that one partner or the other should serve from a particular end rather than that you should open with your stronger service game.

Where a pair's service games are of about equal strength no matter which player is serving, the decision about who shall serve first should normally be governed by weather conditions alone.

The sun mainly affects pairs containing a left-hander. For both players to avoid the sun as much as possible, the left-hander should serve from the southern end in the morning and from the northern end in the afternoon. Strangely enough, at first thought, this applies in either hemisphere.

Advantage can be taken of a crosswind, as when one partner has a strongly curved slice service. A left-hander may use the cross-wind to such good effect that he will prefer to serve from his other-than-normal end.

If the wind is straight up and down the court and the two partners are equally balanced and have no preference for serving downwind or upwind, nothing is affected. If, however, the partners are most unequally balanced (applying mixed doubles again, if you like, as an example of unequal physical strength and net ability), then the weaker player should serve downwind. This adds pace to his service, slows down the return of service he has to take for his first volley, and gives the stronger net-man every chance of exerting his influence on the game.

Other pairs may be balanced in strength but have clear preference for serving ends. One may consist of a fast server who likes to crash his serves downwind and a partner with a twisty serve who likes to twist them up into the wind. Another pair may consist of a fast erratic server who needs to serve into a cushion of wind before he can get many into court and a partner who has enough spin to control the ball downwind. In either of these pairs each partner has a suitable end to serve from.

On a windy day two partners may find that they both badly want the same end. It may be that each really prefers the same side of the court as well. Perhaps the stronger player should always have the choice. Perhaps, in this Scotch mixture of conflicting partners with identical desires, the spoils should be divided. Otherwise if one man were the loser on both counts it might be asking almost too much of him that he should play completely with his partner, never deserting him and never playing against him—till death do them part. The best answer is a rapid dissolution of partnership. In plain words, they are not a pair.

The preceding discussion should not lead you to think that the choice of end is more important that the opportunity to serve first. If you win the toss you should normally choose the serve. There is a decided advantage in being a game ahead with your opponent's service to break over being a game down and your own service to hold. In most cases there is not enough difference in strength between a pair's two service games to warrant giving up this advantage. If the set is short (non-advantage) serving first is even more important.

Only where a pair's service games are unbalanced in strength and where conditions make it most desirable that at least one of the players should serve from a certain end, should the end be chosen in preference to the serve to avoid being forced into opening with your far weaker service game.

Vary what has been said in this chapter to suit yourself, but the net must be taken at every opportunity, and the two players must cover it between them. If two virtual strangers play together, the main thing to settle beforehand is that each will cover his own lobs.

If you and some friend intend setting up in business as a regular doubles pair, do not make the mistake of thinking the whole thing is entirely a matter of position. Position plays a large part, but you should never forget that strokes are still the fundamentals of your game, in singles or in doubles. The whole idea of gaining command with your first volley and taking control of the subsequent play can come apart at its very seams if you cannot be sure of getting your second serves on to the receiver's backhand in the first court. If you had not practiced and developed a reliable overhead, what point would there be in your having the net position and forcing your opponents into difficult situations from which all they could do would be to toss?

CHAPTER TEN

Points — Particular and sundry

Playing the points/Dead spots/Losing/Coaching

Set and match points are in a class by themselves. Apart from these, everyone knows that the most vital points are game points with a difference of only one point in the score. So I cannot argue about it, except perhaps to offer the obvious thought that any score could have been 40-30 instead of 30-40 if one of the earlier points in the game had gone the other way.

Of these less spectacular points, a number of players regard the first as the most important because it puts you in front and means that your opponent has to win two running before he can take that happy position away from you. Some plump for the third point because it puts you within striking distance of a game point. Other insist on the value of winning both the first and third points. You will readily see that you could make a case for each point if you tried.

There can be no quarrel here. All points are valuable, and any theory you devise aids this realization.

Rather grudgingly, I have to admit there are one or two points you can afford to lose. From 40-0, loss of the next point may not be too much of a tragedy. In a hard match with an opponent holding all his serves and then reaching 40-0, although I would take the next point if it came my way I could not say with any conviction that I would tire myself over it in a long defensive rally.

As a general rule, taking them all as being valuable avoids storing up crisis points for yourself, which, you will

Lew Hoad prepares for a high volley . . . (See text, page 100)

Lifts his racket . . .

Stretches for the ball . . .

and makes contact.

The ball heads deep into his opponent's backhand corner.

You can always be confident with high volleys,
provided you are sideways to the net.
(See text, page 100)

remember, is not travelling light. Despite this, you must know the score at all times. Though all points count the same, there is advantage in playing them differently.

In the earlier points you can vary your game somewhat to prevent your opponent from getting to know it too well—although if you are having the better of a rally you should never take any risk that gives him as much as a fifty-fifty chance of getting out of it. But on game points and points one away from a game point you should always play the soundest tactical shot offering—the one from which you can handle his return if he gets the ball back, and not the one which may beat him but, if it doesn't, is quite likely to lose the point for you instead.

Don't surrender games

Players intentionally let a set go now and then if they decide it is past winning, and this is sometimes wiser than tiring yourself to no purpose. If you decide to throw a set, you should keep your own shots in order rather than play weakly and let your opponent get in some confidence-building stroke practice for the opening of the next set. What I have in mind, however, is mistakenly letting a game go in a set you are trying to win.

Even hardened competitors are sometimes guilty of this. In plain terms, players seem to lose patience with a game and would rather start a new one. For example, a player has a lead of 30-40 on his opponent's serve, gets on top in a long rally, but finally loses it against a lucky shot; at deuce he misses one he should not have; his opponent then gets a first serve in and the player makes no attempt to battle it out as he did a few moments before at 30-40: instead he attempts a reckless hit-or-miss winner, mentally losing the point even before he hits the ball, and decides he will get back on the job in the next game. Another similar instance is where a player gets fed-up on his own service game and you see him end it with a double-fault which, if it was not deliberate, was at least uninterested.

Writing off a messed-up game in order to start again with a clean sheet must be one of our natural reactions because it is done so often. The player thinks he is cutting his losses and starting again with a fresh mind. But he is not cutting his losses, for there was no need to have given the game up. Except for a long game of many deuces, which is comparatively rare and cannot be foreseen, in any game in which a point or two has already been played you are actually fewer points away from winning that game than you can ever be in a new one.

You should ignore the fact that your opponent is also nearer to winning in the game being played. If you don't, you are adopting a statistician's outlook rather than a tennis-player's. Whatever you are at other times, while you are playing tennis you are a tennis-player.

The mistake in thinking that you will be better off with a new game really lies in your worrying over past errors in the present game. You may be starting the new game with a fresh mind, but did you really need this mental rest for which the price was a forfeited game? All that's really happening is that in your impatience you are temporarily losing concentration.

Purposeless ground shots

Noticeable dead spots sometimes occur in your game, even if your standard is quite high. Most of these can be overcome merely by knowing about them. Here they are then:

• Playing a short one for no reason in the middle of a rather uneventful rally.

• Lapsing into almost nothing in a tense final set when your opponent slows the game down and obviously invites errors with a "come and get me" attitude.

• Vaguely playing for depth.

• Sidelining the net-man in doubles but hitting the ball over the baseline.

In most of these situations the trouble lies in our tending to regard our opponent's territory as a large amount of empty paddock; even with the doubles sideline shot we tend to think only of the opening and not of the restricting baseline.

If the idea helps you, divide your opponent's court into six large squares: say, short forehand, backhand, and center; deep forehand, backhand, and center. In an uneventful rally, never play a ball into the short center square, for this is very often the beginning of the eventual loss of that rally.

Against the slowed-down game, instead of either pressing when you are tense or being at a complete loss what to do, play the ball as calmly as your opponent is playing it, but with the aim of sending it into one of the three deep squares; you can then await the most suitable of any one of his succession of nothing-shots to place awkwardly and advance to the net. This applies in all cases where neither of you wishes to attack; a particular instance could be where your opponent is down four-five on his service and you feel you can probably handle him provided you do not gamble things away. Using the deep squares makes you feel you are doing something positive.

Hitting to the deep squares is the same as playing for length, but when you do this while using the backline as your guide you seem to hit a lot of balls just in and too many just out. Deep squares may not give an immaculate length, but they will always help you to aim on the right side of the baseline.

When sidelining in doubles, aim for the deep corner square. It may not be a personal weakness of yours, but many players, when they concentrate on outwitting the net-man, do seem to hit the ball towards infinity.

Losing

Losing matches is not the aim of this book, but one or two points about it are worth mentioning.

People are right when they say that they do not mind losing a good game; it is playing badly and throwing it away that they hate. Sound strokes, not hopes, fears and post-mortems, are the only answer to this worry. They ensure that you will seldom lose to an inferior player (in singles, anyway, though doubles can have some uncanny twists), and that against stronger players you will nearly always play as well as you are allowed. No longer will you ever fear defeat. It will come when it comes, but you will not fear it. Your pre-match outlook will improve out of sight.

At the same time you should avoid resigning yourself to a more or less contented loss while you are still in the process of putting up a reasonable performance. Time and again you see a man one set down (quite a good one) and serving at four-five and losing it almost complacently because he feels satisfied with being far from disgraced.

In these circumstances it is better to look at it more like this: It is your serve—you have an even-money chance, so try hard for the first point. If you win that game—five-all, even chance of the set. If you win the set—set-all, even chance for the match (and better than even, because most three-set matches are won by the winner of the second set). I know these are not bookmakers' odds, because three even-money chances do not add up to a combined even-money result. But I maintain that they are the only odds a tennis-player should recognize.

Never inwardly settle with yourself before a game that you would be well satisfied if you got, say, three games in each set. Settle for nothing in advance. In action, look towards winning the point you are playing or about to play. If you have never tried it before, you may be very well pleased to find how much more you enjoy the game.

Older players, already having the advantage of experience on their side when they play young opponents, should never resort to tricks to avoid defeat. Some members of the old brigade imagine their tricks to be devious; in fact they are mostly obvious and sometimes degrading. Never stall for time; a young opponent will always allow you to have it.

Whatever the reason for his defeat—a hot day, a pro-tracted match, an old muscle injury, etc.—an old-timer should never mention age when congratulating the victor, even if his own strokes are still superior. It does neither side any good and in some circumstances can be annoying. No one makes a good impression when he cries age. Until you have retired—when you are entitled to remember only your halcyon days—your present form is your only form. Losing when possibly you should have won may be a little difficult to take at first. Don't despair. After a while you'll find yourself getting plenty of practice at it.

The value of coaching

Coaches in the main are knowledgeable and dedicated men who give value for money. They now adapt their methods and advice for varying types of players. Gone are the days when anyone could say that so-and-so had been a promising player with a crop of natural shots until a coach forced him to alter his style and left him with nothing at all. Modern coaches teach orthodox Eastern-type strokes to beginners, and with advanced players they try to replace unorthodox weaknesses with stronger orthodox techniques. Orthodoxy does not mean being restricted; on the contrary, it is the foundation that offers the greatest scope for future development. When coaches find a natural strength already developed in a player they usually encourage it, whether it is strictly orthodox or not.

Gone, too, are the days when a man could justifiably say that if his son were to be coached then he wanted a very good coach and not any old one who happened to be about. Rather than quote certificates and qualifications I will rely on the deliberate understatement that all coaches know quite a little more than their pupils.

Advanced players do not go to coaches nearly enough. Their games go to pieces every now and then, and off the court they shake their heads in puzzlement and disbelief: "I don't know. Can't understand it. Don't know what's the matter," and so on. Well, instead of spending the money on some other form of solace why not visit someone who can understand and does know exactly what is the matter?

If you do go to a coach you should should be careful

not to expect too much. He will remedy any specific weakness you take to him and thereby improve your general game, but a few lessons from him will not automatically make you district champion. Fair is fair. A visit or two to a doctor cures an ailment; it doesn't turn you into a Hercules.

You should not get into the frame of mind, much less the habit, of relying too much on the coach. Listen, watch, and try-out, but decide for yourself what you are going to accept. It is your game, not the coach's. In your next match it is you who will be playing, not he. Even if you are a junior receiving regular coaching you must still take the responsibility of looking after yourself; otherwise you will become too self-conscious and too coach-conscious if he watches one of your matches.

Do not decide too hastily that you have gone to the wrong shop or that you have outgrown your present coach if you find you can defeat him in singles. With experience, coaches become increasingly competent in stroke production and fault correction, but because they are always watching their pupils instead of the ball their own play falls off. Anyhow, world champions have to get their coaching from men they can beat.

If you accept the view that a satisfactory match temperament stems from satisfactory strokes, you may also agree that coaching is the most direct means of getting the foundation of those strokes. Actually getting them, of course, will depend entirely on yourself, and it is here that no one can hold your hand for you.

Fitter than you think

You need to be fit, and most players are much fitter than they think they are. Champions do exercises and road work, but weekend players need little more than their weekly game. Avoid getting fat; it is a great handicap, and exercise hardly takes it off. Find out what food is the cause and eat less of it.

If you become breathless on the court, do not imagine

it is the end, and don't take deep breaths to cure it. Take quick shallow ones (dogs have set an example we have been slow to follow) and you will be over it in a point or two.

People under thirty-five seldom really need a rest before the third set. You may be very hot and there may be some mental tension, but it is mostly only a habit. Physically, you seldom really need it. Nothing will make you so tired as thinking that you might be. Leave it to your opponent to think he's the one who's tired.

Trifles are only trifles

So much has been said in this book about fine points and picking up small advantages here and there that I hope I haven't conveyed the wrong idea that every little thing is of great importance. You should learn to distinguish between what really matters in a game and what are mere trifles that must not be allowed to put you off.

Trifles can be of our own making or merely accidental. You may have forgotten your shoes and have had to borrow a pair that do not fit well. You may break a string and have to continue with a borrowed racket of different weight. You may be playing an opponent whose supporters applaud every point that goes his way, including those he does not really win, such as when you miss a smash or serve a double-fault.

Here is a way of testing whether anything is a trifle or not: If it happened to your opponent instead of to you, would it be really likely to make you win the match?

Beware of letting trifles affect you. It is a form of self-pity, or close to it anyway. And self-pity is a dangerous luxury which no would-be winner can afford to have anywhere near him.

"An ornament to the game"

Perhaps this is the way you would like to be described. Casting any cynicism aside, if it were genuinely said of you, you probably would be most pleased. Praise from sportsmen is not lightly given. You are not likely to gain such high regard—few players do—but it is possible.

Suitable assets of the more apparent kind are a sunny disposition, impressive or popular manner, elegant strokes, being one of Nature's gentlemen, etc. But none of these is essential.

Here is a formula. Never regard bad sportsmanship or any sort of "performing" as colorful. In "incidents," do not try to play even the hero's part. Make no flamboyantly sporting gestures, overshadowing your opponent. Call correctly, and indulge in no tricks.

When you win, never walk off and leave your opponent behind. If the match had been a real battle you would buy him a drink, walk over with him to his friends, or whatever the circumstances called for. Do the same sort of thing after any win, especially when you have won rather easily. This helps to take away any sting of disappointment your opponent may be feeling. When you lose, tell your opponent he was too good—without any qualifications whatsoever. To anyone else, make no excuses at all and limit discussion of the reasons for your loss to those who ask. There should be no visible savageness, sulkiness, or moodiness.

Play hard in all conditions. Make your own share of winners instead of living off the mistakes of others. Never haul down your flag—make opponents of your own standard feel they always have to fight hard to beat you.

And turn up again next Saturday.

CHAPTER ELEVEN

Parting shots

I cannot presume to say that everything I have written is right and bears no argument. I can only say that it is the way I have found things to be in tournament play over many years.

What is important is what you yourself have found in this book. If you have read all of it, then, like the baffled physician who finally prescribed two or three days' rest in bed, I shall feel safe enough in saying it should do you no harm.

Anything that you decide applies directly to yourself, however, should be thoroughly known and practiced on the court until it becomes part of your game. Forget that it may have come from this book. Regard it as your own, as something you picked up along your own way. Left-handers, a self-reliant lot, can gain just as much as any right-hander from the various discussions of their possible strengths and weaknesses and of tactics that might be used against them.

Clearly, winning has been the book's main theme. Almost every aspect of the game has been examined to see if it contributed to that end. Even a sacrosanct ideal like sportsmanship has here and there been made to pay toll.

Well, that was the stated aim, but it is now time to pay a plain tribute to sportsmanship. I believe that somewhere along the road all tennis players come to realize that the sportsmanship encountered in others and developed in oneself is alone sufficient reason for playing.

Strokes are the ultimate basis of winning tennis. For this reason my book has been dedicated to Jack Crawford, the player I regard as having handled a racket better than anyone I saw, anywhere, over a period of about forty years.

You may be a most impressive-looking gentleman with a crop of long musician's hair, you may have a wonderfully calm manner, and you may know exactly the right position to stand on the stage—but you cannot very well give a violin concert if you cannot play a note.

When experimenting with new strokes, never forget to end your practice with some of your old stand-bys. Far too many balls are hit unnecessarily into the net. Even if your last errors have been outs your motto for every next shot should be "Low—and *Past the Net*."

I am ready to admit that somewhere in the world someone is playing his high volleys square-on to the net and not hooking them over the sideline. Perhaps he has the wrong foot forward as well. Perhaps they are his favorite shots, and at this moment he may even be ending his crazy practice with some of them.

I also accept that now and then this book falls into the confident tone adopted by retired players who, having no more tests to face themselves, have a bland answer for everything an opponent could possibly do. However, I stick to my optimistic guns in saying that a tennis player's aim should be to secure the advantage to himself in anything that happens. This attitude is a much greater aid to him than odd pieces of luck such as winning the toss or getting a number of net-cords and liners.

There is no need for anyone to give way to excessive nervousness. Nervousness is always partial, never complete. Sitting in a dentist's waiting-room, we may sometimes be too nervous to read a magazine article properly, but at least we can manage to look at the pictures. In a match, nervousness can prevent us from playing with confidence, but it need not stop us from hitting easy shots into court.

Always try to *enjoy* your tennis. Playing the tightest match without a smile and at maximum concentration, you should still enjoy it. Leaving all pleasantries aside, if you have only your opponent to beat instead of yourself as well, you are giving yourself a better chance.

May I make my final attack on temperament?

With compliments from Harry Hopman to Rosie Casals at Kooyong. Never dwell on a victorious ending while playing. (See text, page 14)

U.S. L.T.A. photogr

Two of the game's ornaments. (See text, pages 181–2)

Decide whether to have it round your neck like pure lead or to replace it with an amalgam composed of sound strokes, known purpose, and complete absorption. If temperament is neither physical nor hereditary, then it follows that you have a freer choice in the matter than you may have imagined.

You may find, some time after you have begun working on your game in accordance with this book, that you are sounder, that you have won some close matches you might formerly have lost, that you are now more confident of always beating those players you should be able to beat, and that in general your ideas work when you have control of the game . . . nevertheless, whenever someone is too good for you, you will find that your tactics cannot be brought to bear and that some of your shots break up as well.

That, I'm afraid, is life in the tennis world. When you are overmatched it is too much to expect that all your strokes will be fireproof. What we all have to do is get better so that fewer players will overmatch us and in more matches we can get that feeling of being in control. This is supposed to be a hard grind, but after half a century of preference for playing games rather than working all the time, I don't think it is.

For those who like nothing better than beautiful simplicity in all things, here is an interesting thought. We have found that temperament has no more than its place, that misdemeanors from unworthy gamesmanship to deliberate cheating do not really pay, and that the basic ingredients of success lie in concentration and sound stroke technique. In other words, the game can best be won by a keen sportsman and his racket. That, no doubt, was exactly what the inventors of tennis intended, years and years ago.

The methods by which our sportsman and his racket achieve their success I have attempted to suggest in this book. My last parting shot, therefore, is to sketch the general picture of the type of thought I have tried to convey:

- Practice your strokes till they are grooved, and know

the game, and in play you will be free to concentrate on the ball.

• Regard the dimensions of the court as being most reasonable, so that the easiest place to hit most shots is into the court.

• Look on volleying as being as natural as catching a ball, and therefore go into volley whenever you feel you can cover the net.

• Force your opponent to lob as much as possible, being confident that if you handle each lob with the degree of respect it deserves you are in a winning position.

• On long shots (service and ground strokes) stop the ball, hit the racket center, and send the ball past the net.

• Play for each point. Vary your game to limit an opponent's anticipation, but from 30-15 or 15-30 onwards keep to the soundest tactical shot.

None of this makes the game dull; it is only from a sound basis that those countless and varying combinations of shots and positions can develop.

If your opponent cannot prevent you from getting your weight into the ball and hitting the center of your racket, then expect to win. If he is preventing you, change the game. Always continue your efforts until after the last point; who knows, his game may deteriorate, and the match practice is well worth the effort.

When badly overmatched, never descend to weak dejection or loss of interest; play as strongly as you can and keep your self-respect. You may earn your opponent's and the gallery's respect as well, but that is not as important.

I have had my say and would like to make an abrupt ending. I wouldn't like anyone to think I wanted to talk for as long as I have played.

Index